# Indian Curry with German Beer

# Indian Curry with German Beer

## Life Between Indian-German Culture

Dr.G

PARTRIDGE
A Penguin Random House Company

**To order additional copies of this book, contact**
Partridge India
000 800 10062 62
orders.india@partridgepublishing.com

www.partridgepublishing.com/india

# PREFACE

If you are holding this book, probably you are the one who is about to visit Germany or the one who is already in Germany or the one who is looking out for a funny story behind the title 'Indian Curry with German beer.' Welcome onboard! The journey you are about to take is full of fun, joy, and entertainment. The book promises to leave you with hours of laughter, excitement and eagerness to experience the Indo-German cultural shocks. So, fasten your seat belts we are about to take off!

How I decided to write this book…

Late in the evening, on my rocking chair and with my soul mate I was enjoying Germany's the most scenic view, the sunset in summer. The sky was covered with the pinkish-red hue, which till date overrule my wife's beauty.

We were enjoying our favorite meal - homemade Indian Curry with the German beer sitting in the balcony. I recalled my journey from 23 years young Indian lad to a 33 years old global fellow. I was recollecting my memories, my stay in Germany and, of course, and the intercultural clashes. Remembering everything left us with hours of laughter and giggle. She knew almost all the things happened to me while I was trying to attune myself to the newly welcomed German culture. It was total fun hours of recalling. We didn't even realize how the time passed. Sooner it was, and we still didn't want to stop discussing my fun journey and the experiences. There was no end to that conversation. It continued next day too.

While hopping from one country to another, its cultural differences, at times, becomes a bitter pill to swallow. Coming from India, adjusting oneself with German culture becomes a challenge. Till date, I have experienced ample of funny cultural shocks that are worth communicating. There is a whole list of 'do's' and 'don'ts' that one needs to follow. Of course, it is not mandatory, but it is good if one is aware of it; at least to enjoy Indian curry with German beer with peace of mind!

Sharing my experiences, I started advising my Indian friends and became 'German Culture Guru' among my peers. Of course, I was not a Guru! However, my tips helped my friends a lot, and hence the title. I don't mind the title, though! I still had no plans writing a book!

I was at the Frankfurt Airport where I read a line that inspired me to break the ice. It says,

**"If you don't find a right book, it's your duty to write one."**

It was then I decided to pen my experience on paper so that it can reach out maximum people giving them a clear picture Germany culture. It will be fun for Germans to know how Indians sees their culture. The challenges I faced, the shocks I absorbed, fun I had, friends I made, and on the top Tips I wrote, I decided to jot it down. Whatever I have experienced in the last ten years in Germany, I summarized all in this entertaining book.

This book is about real intercultural incidents that I faced in Germany. All the incidents illustrated are in a form of short stories, and let me tell you, stories are funny, humorous and entertaining. Each story is not less than a movie scene. The book contains golden rules and tips for an Indian in Germany as well as for a German in India. Book is to understand, feel, learn and enjoy the German culture. It is a handbook for Indian employees, business partners, students, travelers and visitors in Germany.

**Dr.G**

# ACKNOWLEDGEMENT

To whom I should thank and to whom I should express gratitude? Ooh it's a tough Call! As the numbers are too high and cannot write all names. Therefore, every single person with whom I met in Germany helped me to collect the intercultural information and to summarize in this book. Thanks to all!

Cheers to other writers, who didn't write this book, so that I got that chance to write.

I am grateful to my parents who brought me into this world and made in "One in the billion". Indeed, they never wanted me to go to Germany but my stubborn nature helped me to convince them by throwing tantrums on them. It works only with parents, not with the wife.

Oh! About my wife, special thanks to her who motivated me to get break. I got a good reason to spend a peaceful time to write.

Apart from jokes, Big thanks to all my university friends, hostel friends, digital friends (social media friends), colleagues, Professors, mentors, publishing team and the readers. Imagining this journey without YOU is an impossible task for me.

THANKS A LOT!

# TEAM

| | |
|---|---|
| Idea and concept work | *Prashant Dogra, Karuna Syal (my wife) Dharmesh Sheta, Hetal Sheta and YESGERMANY Education team* |
| Mentor | *Pawan Mishra and Tarun Sharma* |
| Illustrations | *Sumit Sahani* |
| Writing and Editing | *Gaganpreet Kaur and Lavina bhambhani* |
| Proofreading | *Namita Breja* |
| Text Evaluation | *Prachi Mangal, Darpan Syal, Rakesh Raja and Pradeep Somanahalli.* |
| Content Advisor | *Beate Renninger, Manuel Kimmerle, Saba Paloji, Shivani Syal, Surekha Sharma, Vinay Sharma, Shailja Sharma, Puneet Chug, Gagan Dhand, Dr. Abhishek Kumar, Ashish Dahad, Ashish Sethi, Wahhid Sabir, Urvarshi Thareja, Ashok Kumar, Vivek Khariwal, Varun Garg, Julia Zinsmeister, Setia family and Syal family.* |
| Publishing | *Yanessa Evans and Pohar Baruah Partridge – The Penguin Random House* |

# Contents

# 1.  BEFORE FLY

*Leaving Indian social comedy*

$B$eing a die-hard fan of Michael Schumacher and Bruce Willis, and a worshipper of Albert Einstein, it was my dream to come to Germany for further studies.

*Ah, whom am I kidding?*

I wanted to come to Germany to lead a tech-savvy life and to see its luxurious cars zooming past me. Also, the great Oktoberfest and its famous big 1-liter beer called Mass. Apart from this, I just wanted to get away from home. I chose Germany as an option as I did not have prying relatives at every corner in Germany like I had in America, where all my relatives were breeding like bunnies all over the country. Germany had good options, excellent courses, no tuition fee and appealing opportunities for international students, and I was all geared up for it.

The incident, which I am narrating, had happened to me before I flew to Germany for further studies. I still remember each and every second of that day as if it is still plastered in my eyes. The sun was shining bright and golden, and yet it was not all that hot because it rained like crazy just two days ago, and I could still feel the moisture in the air. I can remember every second of it like Sherlock Holmes film's flashback, where he knows the color of neighbor's daughter's pet dog's favorite teddy's shoe's lasses. The moment I saw my Visa Stamp from German Embassy Delhi, I started jumping right outside the German embassy like a dog that has been given a roll of sausages after being on a diet of Gujarati food for a month.

My happiness knew no bounds, and I felt that I can do anything, right then and right there. It wasn't only the happiness that was enveloping me the most but it was also the dread, a slow but sure feeling that was creeping from the outer skin of my body to the very soul inside. It appeared to me as a dream, I wanted someone to pinch and make me feel that it's all happening in reality. I was so busy with admission, visa documents, interviews, and other tedious paper work that I did not get any time to sit and reflect on the changes that would happen to me.

It was Party time, celebration time, goosing time, bye bye time! However, the very next second I was scared about the change, and this was when it felt real. I was feeling all the emotions that I did not even know existed - Anxiety, tension, panic, unease, apprehension, fear, nervousness!

*Oh, God!* I am sure a small part of my head exploded right outside the embassy and fell on the concrete used to pave outside. And all that happened in fractions of seconds, the freshness of my face drained, and I was this wreck that was just standing there, all helpless. That day I realized the speed of imagination and thinking.

Visa news spread to my entire family and friends like a Virus in computer. In 2006, digital social media was not common, still it reached like a breaking news.

The next thing, my so-called "well-wishers" neighbor, friends and relatives, who had not spoken to me from the time I was a little sperm were contacting me. They were bombarding me with questions of all sorts. I heard and answered questions for which I had no answer for, and I had not even thought of till that moment. Instead of calming me down, those people and their question, ended up increasing my apprehension and foreboding about the journey that I was about to embark upon. Wherever I went, I could only hear,

*"Are you going to GERMANY?"*

*"Why not Amrikaa or Anngland or Kanedaa, you know I have many relatives there?" (My Aunts from Punjab)*

*"Will you come back or are you planning to settle in Germany?"*

*"Do you know somebody there?"*

*"Why you didn't tell us before."*

Though I was a little shaken, my parents did not ask yet any question. I thought to act aloof and not thinking so much about them. But it actually helped me to answer. So, I started answering everyone's questions with confidence that I did not even know existed inside me. Some of those queries and much of the constant prying that was happening were out of genuine concern and well-being for me, but some of it, was just nosey interruptions.

I just shut everybody down by telling them that I am flying, and going away to the land of Engineers (of course it was Beer in my mind!), and that's it. It was finalized and none of those nasty family things would affect me in any way.

The most important part was my parents and family. The entire street filled with my extended family had to be told about my decision. As final decision has to be from family. Not my personal decision! And did I mention that it is a typical joint family? And when I say joint family, let me give a picture of how and where I live.

My dad, along with 5 of his brothers, and their family, live on the same street in adjacent houses. So, that is like 5 families, along with mine, and their extended families as well. Not to mention far too many cousins than I can count. And this is when the chain reaction started. I had told just my parents that I had decided to go abroad for further studies. Finally, my father and uncles appreciated my decision and gave me green signal to go to Germany. And, before I knew about this decision, the entire street (my family) was coming over with their kids as they had found out about final news.

Trust me, I never thought that I would see so many emotions surrounding me in all my life. I used to watch the TV serial (also known as daily soaps) after coming back from school, sitting with my mother. But, I never expected to see my whole family behaving like the characters out of a daily soap.

The questions never stopped. My family, consisting of human beings, was suddenly behaving like an Examination Question Bank. And of course, most of the questions were about food.

*"What will you eat there?"*

*"Can you cook, how will you manage?"*

*"Does Germany have a lot of Indians?"*

*"ooooh. Alcohol and Cow meat will also be there, right?"*

*"Promise us, you will not marry white girl."*

And they never stopped. I realized that if I just sit there and smile, I can get through this exam that they were putting me through. While all the elder members of the family were concerned about food, the younger cousins all had a whole different idea – about cars, beers and blond girls.

It was during this time that I realized how much my family loves me, and needs me. It was during this period that I actually started feeling the love that they had for me. I realized that being in a joint family, everybody, right from my uncles to aunts loved me to death, and it was this love, that they were showing in their questions.

I am sure it is new for a non-Indian, but for an Indian it is normal and the same culture is reflected in our business too. Even in corporate, we know colleagues and their families. That's why Indians can ask personal questions even in the first meeting.

My mother had already started crying and sobbing and giving me impromptu hugs whenever she could find me. I tried to explain that I was not going for a war, its just another country for further studies! Slowly, with each passing day, she came to terms with the fact that I was about to leave. The love that a mother has for her child is pure, and I understood it that day. Soon the feeling that I would miss my home, the place where I grew up and spent my entire childhood, the place where I completed my education, the place where all my friends are, crept in. I started seeing things in a different way, my tidy room, my dog "Jacky," my bike "bullet," billiards club "Snooker" etc. I was spending time and wanted to grab all that moments in my hand and there were times, when I used to break down suddenly.

And then it was D-day! The day had come when I had to fly to Germany and had to live all alone. My flight was late at night, and right from the day before that particular day, all of the relatives started coming over to say the last goodbye, or to share some last minute news.

On the day I had to fly to Germany, just before I could get into the car to go to the airport, there were no less than 30 members in my house just so that they could see me go. It was a very memorable day for me, seeing all the people I love at a single place. Our narrow street was full of my family members and passing by neighbors were also stopping and saying bye to me.

It was night 9 pm, dark night, with some broken street lights, friends, relatives, cousins, neighbors, everybody was there! And there was a different kind of excitement in the air that day.

Now, the big question was, who all will be coming with me to the airport? Only a typical Indian can understand the importance of this issue. With a lot of convincing, and a lot of shouting involved, we had cut down a lot of members and finally decided who all are going to be there. After all the shortlisting there were still three cars full of family members who would accompany me to the airport. So, it was going to be me, my parents, and my brother in one car, my friends in 2nd car, and my sister and her husband in the 3rd car.

Another big question was, which car will I travel in? Everybody wanted to spend as much time with me as possible. And finally, we reached a decision that I will be going with my sister, and brother-in-law. (brother-in-law is the most important person in joint family – Indian tradition), this decision had a logical reason as well. My brother-in-law had travelled a lot, and I was shoved into this car as they wanted him to give me tips, in that one-hour ride to the airport.

Although my mind was saturated, I went along with whatever they said! Germany was probably the last thing on my mind at that time., and I was just thinking about how much I am going to miss this place and my friends. I had apprehensive about the place I was traveling to. A place about which I had no clue about, a place I had never been to, a place I have never seen except in videos...

And with all these thoughts in my mind, and with innumerable hugs, and a little more emotional drama at home, I was finally going to ...

A land of Ideas,

A land of Cars,

A land of Engineers,

A land of Autobahn,

A land of Beer,

A land of Oktoberfest,

A land of Sausages,

A land of Bread and Bakery,

A land of Black forest cake (my favorite one),

A land of Alpes, or

Simply a land for ME !

# 2.  TRAVEL TO TALLIPUT

*Dreams come true ............*
*but..............not for me!*

Finally, after all that drama with my typical Indian family, we all managed to reach the airport. Then it was another session of suggestions and advice and more tears. And, some more tears. And then, a few more.

Honestly, I must admit it! I rather loved all the attention that I was getting. My friends were also expressing their feelings, and were telling me how much they would miss me. And I was frankly surprised to hear all that! Those idiots, whom I used to spend most of my time with and do the most stupid things that one could imagine, loved me so much. I was going to miss them too

As the boarding time came near my excitement level also rose. It was partly because I was going away on my own, and partly because it was my first flight. I was excited about the flight. It was not an expression but my inner emotions were the same when I got my first cycle in childhood.

I had heard from my other rich friends who had been on flights and who had gone to other countries for vacations that one gets fabulous and exotic food on the flight. In addition, one even gets endless alcohol! My happiness was beyond limits - Free alcohol! That too thousand feets above the ground? I was waiting for that all my life!

I got into the flight, and saw that there were some gorgeous airhostesses. I was waiting for the little toffees and candies that the airhostesses bring in. But, hey! Please don't judge me. Everybody loves free stuff or tiny little chocolates that we get in flights. I was ready and waiting for the king like the treatment that I was about to get. And little did I know that my happy bubble was about to get burst my deal traditional airlines. Finally, a beautiful airhostess came to me and asked.

*What would you like to drink? Juice or Coke?*

Hey, Coke! I can get them at the store next to my house! But I had decided on taking some juice, because I thought that it is much more exotic that coke. I thought it's just a welcome drink and alcohol will come later. So, I opted for the much fascinating apple juice. But, I ended up getting tetra pack, which, by the way, tasted nothing like how I expected it to feel like. I found out later on that the apple juice is considered good for nothing in Europe. No wonder I ended up not liking it!

The food was like kids menu. I never asked for the alcohol, because the airhostess was too lovely and I was too shy to go up to her and ask her for some booze. She must have thought that I am a kid, which I was. So, I ended up with kid's treatment.

Next to me was this potbellied 40-something guy who started a conversation with me, which I wholeheartedly wanted to avoid. He had asked me so many questions that he could write my biography. He found out a lot about me in that long flight to Germany, but I could only find out one thing about him. And it was the fact that he was not wearing clean socks. And do I need to go into the details of how annoying and choking it is to have a person wearing stinking socks inside a closed box that is flowing a few thousand feet above the ground? The entire way during the journey, all I could think of was his socks. Imagine, this was my first flight, and it was clearly not a very happy, or at least, a very fragrant experience.

I did not understand if all of those fairy tales that I was told about flight travel were fake. Being the unfortunate person that I am, was having all of these issues with my first ever flight!

The rest of the flight went on without any incidents happening around me. I flew from Delhi to Berlin and with connecting flight to Hannover. And before I knew it, I was in Hannover, Germany! My destination was here, and when I was getting down from the flight, I felt a different kind of excitement surging through me. I was shaking with nerves, or excitement, or maybe it was just too cold over there, I still do not know. The shivering was right in my bones, and I did not know what lay ahead in my endeavors here. But I was prepared for it.

I had watched a lot of movies before I came down here, and I noticed that all the heroes kiss the ground no matter what. And after stepping in Germany, I also wanted to do the same, and I expected my eyes to become wet. Nothing of that sort happened, and if I had done the whole scene of kissing the earth, then I am sure people would have taken me for a lunatic.

My German friends from the university whom I had met through some contact had come to the airport to pick me up. I saw them for the first time and they were waiting for me outside the airport.

*When I saw them, I was shocked at first!*

They looked more like models than students who had come to pick me. They were tall. Taller than six and a half foot, with broad shoulders, they were dwarfing me, and I was looking like some kid standing between them. I was truly intimidated by them, and when I finally reached them, they extended their hand, and I shook it. And I swear two of my hands could fit in one of their palms. Shoe size, which doesn't exist in India. Huge, heavy hands are in the genes of this country I guess, as everywhere I looked, I could see that everyone was built along the same lines.

When we started walking towards the parking where Marcel had parked his car, I started feeling like Gulliver on one of his adventurous travels. Gulliver in "Biggiput" or "Talliput". I was looking at other and it seems that I am the smallest among them. Back home, my build was considered above average with 5.6 feet, but here, I could see that everyone was towering over me In India. Here I truly felt like "Chotu". Don't be surprise after I become good of them they were calling me "Kleiner" – means "Chotu" (they still call me "Kleiner").

One thing I recognized later when they asked me,

*"Is it cold for you?"*

It was September with 22°C and I was wearing big jacket with woolen cap as for me 22° in day time is pretty cold and they were in summer clothes in shorts and T-shirts.

Both my friends, Marcel and Alf, were very warm and welcoming. They were my first friends in Germany, and we remain good friends till date. They took me out, and showed me around and introduced me to the other people around the university. I smiled cordially, and was still not comfortable with all the new people that I was meeting.

Marcel and Alf could talk basic English, and we used to communicate with each other through that basic English. Slowly, I started adapting to the new crowd and the new environment around me.

We went out for lunch, and we found one McDonald's outlet right near our hostel and we thought that we would just have our lunch there. At last McD, where I can eat as normal. In flight with kids menu was nothing and the food was not of my type. I was waiting for my turn to order big menu with Paneer Spicy Burger.

Now, here starts the culture difference not about the taste of food. I thought that I should offer to pay for the food to my friends, as they have taken care of me. When I offered to pay for their food, I received some confused expressions. I was bewildered, as I did not have a clue about what I just said.

Marcel and Alf told me that I do not have to pay for their food, so I ended up thinking that they will pay for my food. However, they did not. This was when I realized that pay for own food here, and the bills are separated. Back home, whenever I used to go out with my friends or family, it was a courtesy to offer to pay for their food as well. I was very much accustomed to this custom and tradition as my entire family, that lives on one street, used to go out together, and usually most of them would insist on paying for the food of the whole family. Even when I used to go out with my cousins, me, being the oldest, would pay the bill.

I had taken these crisp, new Euros with me, and I took out a five hundred Euro note, and gave it to the cashier there at the McDonald's outlet. The cashier over there gave me the weirdest look ever, as the burger and the fries that I had bought for myself must have cost around three Euros or so, and I ended up giving him a five hundred Euro. I thought that in India, I will be given the remaining money back. Little did I know that that was not going to happen.

In simpler words, it is like going to a street vendor selling peanuts in India and giving him a thousand rupee note, and expecting some change back. The same thing happened to me over there.

I realized that five hundred Euros is a significant amount, and it is not like how we treat a five hundred rupee note in India, which when you go out to an outlet like McDonald's, you end up spending the entire amount. Five Hundred Euros is actually equal to as much as thirty-five thousand rupees in Indian currency! I also figured that it is high time I stop converting all of the foreign exchange to the Indian currency and finding out the value. I ended up paying for my burger and fries with smaller bills, and went to see the rest of Germany.

Guys dropped me to my hostel which was a mix of girls and boys. I took a shower and informed my parents that I reached safely. I started roaming around the city and watching the streets, buildings, houses and I realized that the painting we used to make in childhood was of

Germany. Long green field, hut type houses and smoke was coming from Hut, Cristal Clear Street, no dust and clear water in river etc. Which I never experienced scene in hometown.

I went for a quick grocery as it was Saturday evening and on Sundays grocery stores are closed. I realised that most of the things are automatic. They replace people by machines. In that grocery center, I took known stuffs like milk, yoghurt, bread, pasta, coke, and ofcourse beer and went to counter to pay. Shopping was same like in India, but at the counter after paying I was waiting that she will pack my grocery in a bag as in India.

*But she said "what you want".*

*I replied "please pack my stuffs".*

She looked at me in a weird way. I didn't understand the reason of such reaction. People behind me were also telling to move. I didn't understand the situation.

Than one of the person behind me told that

*"Dear, you have to pack your grocery by your own and if you need packing bags, you have to pay".*

*"What and why"* I replied in a baffling way.

But I had no other option and I observed that all other persons were packing their grocery by own and then I learned the German way do-it-yourself.

This was my first day in Germany, and I knew that things had just begun for me.

# 3.   SWIMMING

*If you wear it, you lose it!*

To settle quickly to Germany, I was searching for sport and social activities where I can meet other international students and can make new friends. For those activities, I seek all the prospects given to me from university. I got 100s of prospects about the city, tourism, insurances, hospitals, shopping, clubs, etc.

While attuning myself, one of the pamphlets elicited my attention. Its label penned in bold pink color that says 'Homosexuals in University' surprised me. It is something extraordinary for an Indian to digest. There was hardly any room to house homosexuality in India; no doubt nowadays unofficially it has, earlier it wasn't.

In India, marrying your girlfriend or just being into a relationship (with a girl) is considered as an unprecedented success, as there are many other issues one has to endure. And, in this, thinking of homosexuality is something like taking a nosedive where, you will end up banging your head without knowing the 'why'.

So, let's come back to the pink leaflet. I discovered that out of forty thousand students, more than four thousand registered homosexuals surrounded me. My eyes ball popped out and other balls too. I dug deeper and bounced off the walls to check more about the less heard, and perhaps, the taboo subject for an Indian.

Here, gays receive warmer reception same as we Indian offer geniality to every guest in the house. We give particular regards; provide exceptional food, unique accommodation and phenomenal stay experience. Yes, this is us; everything has to be over the top for the guests whether or not you like them. Likewise, University also fashions gay festivals, offer unique gay parties, gay credit cards and other exceptional facilities.

In fact, gays receive more respect than we do. Yes, this is my University with its exceptional feature that dangled my mind back and forth with every step I took on the premises. Each step questioned my mind with every new query. There were many 'what ifs' and 'how will' questions.

Finally decided, it's not my cup of tea. Still the topic was in my mind and I was afraid too that I was surrounded by many gays.

After spending too much time on it, I found about swimming and quickly registered online and thought of starting to do from very next day, to shred my family love or called my fat.

The sun was brighter than yesterday, and I decided to go for swimming. Okay, now the to-do list. Towel check, swimsuit check etc. I took my utility bag and went to the poolside. It was huge, bright in color and beautifully embraced by natural plants. For a moment, I doubt and re-check my social clause to confirm whether or not it comes under 'Not Chargeable' clause. The smell of Chlorine water, which I literally hate and cannot ignore.

Indian are very flexible, and I ignored that smell because the place was freaking awesome! The ambiance, pure blue water, lights, people and the aura.

I went as a normal Indian with swimwear and big towel. I hunt for the cabin. But, I could not find any. And, then there was an elongated wall upon which the shower nozzles were mounted. I thought what's harm in taking an open shower? I just had a glance at the students who were already taking the shower. But, when I focused my vision, I was shocked.

*I was standstill*

*It was truly an electric SHOCK! GOOSEBUMPS!*

*The guys were NAKED ! COMPLETELY NAKED!*

They were without a single piece of cloth and more than 10 boys of different age showing their ding-dongs and taking bath.

*Suddenly!*

My mind again got hooked to the 'pink leaflet', and all gay thing was then refreshed. Imagine, a 23-year-old kiddy, little, sweet Indian guy and very new to western culture, I was not able to digest that

*I was surrounded by GAY GROUP!*

I thought unknowingly now I am the part of some gay group or the particular gay swimming time. There was sweat all over my face with fright and anxiety. I felt as if they were trying to ogle me. I was terrified. I felt like a mouse surrounded by big CATs who will catch me within seconds.

Being a boy and confident about German law, I held my emotions and decided to play it cool like "TOM" mouse in Tom & Jerry. I gathered my confidence and without much ado had a shower with swimwear on my 'utensils'. There all were looking at me and seems to laugh at me. I was not able to understand the language and not even their jokes. But I could easily understand that they were talking about me.

As I was new to that area, I was trying to start the shower and adjusting the tap using hit and trial method. Then suddenly, one of the gay was about to get close to me.

*What could I have done?*

Would I find a clever solution and attack like TOM or run to find help?

If I attack, they would not leave me!

*What what what what could I do, my mind was speeding and gearing up like Fomula-1.*

My heartbeat was increasing exponentially, the closer he was coming to my nervousness was growing. He was approaching so fast that I become more impatient. I thought there is something of 'that' kind about to happen. He would hunt me.

I finally decided to use ESCAPE Method. I screamed Bachaoooooo (HELP) and rushed as if I have a fire on my tail to the cabin, covered myself up with basic pullovers, and dashed to my room. I was so quick that I forgot my towel, soap and other stuff in Shower area. Who cares about such tiny stuff when the important is to safeguard one's own prestige.

My hostel was not too far and I rushed towards it. I could easily make world record if someone could measure my speed. I was so fast! On my way to the hostel, I clashed with one boy on the stairs and he tried to save me from falling. I screamed even louder as there was no one on stairs. I reached my room and locked my room. I took a long breath, washed my face and drank water. I was hearing people outside the room talking and laughing on my behavior. Knowing the less, I decided to drop all my plans for the day.

Next day, I discussed the incident with my senior Indian friends. I felt so safe and guarded around them, as if I have got in one of my own cities. I narrate the whole incident word by word.

However, the surprise was to watch them laughing. I wanted to punch them badly, but also eager to know the reason for the 'fantastic' laughter. The meaning of LOL (Laughing out loud) I faced the first time in Germany. They were continuously laughing and falling from beds.

After they were tired of their unusual laugh and one friend said,

*WELCOME TO GERMANY!*

They explained me the shocking German culture. It was then I get to know it comes from standard German culture to have a nude shower. No matter whether with friends,

Professors, brother or even dad, it is very customary to put no clothes during shower. This one cultural shock took almost 15 minutes to recover and took years to digest. The same culture applies to girls also.

It was then I learned...

*You lose it if you wear it!*

Do like what Germans do. And, remember not every naked person taking shower is a GAY!

# 4.   COLLEGE LIFE

*Memories for Lifetime!*

Life continued with such SHOCKS and being an engineer, I was working on how to absorb these shocks.

Indeed, I was enjoying these shocks and the best thing about living in Germany was the time I spent at the University. In India, we are always reminiscing about college life, and we have seen people entering colleges and coming out of them as a whole a completely different person. In Germany, they don't call it "College", but it is just referred as University. In India, we have university and under that university, various affiliated colleges in different cities. But here in Germany it's all in one place and Grand! And I am not kidding when I say this. Indian college where I did my Bachelor was like a Lego land compared to German universities. Wide archways, huge lawns, big buildings are there but sometimes they have monotonous colors - gray or white. Inside design is also not colorful. Most of the furniture is of the same color. Sometimes I feel Germans don't like colors.

The best part is sports Halls. Simply with WAAAW factor! Halls are fully equipped with tools, accessories and trainers for all level at almost negligible cost. The campus of these universities usually includes the hostels and the lecture halls, and there usually are different units for all of the courses. All my dreams of foreign universities, which I imagined due to Hollywood fan, were getting realistic.

I am sure that to take a complete tour of the buildings, it will take me more than a week. Even after I completed my studies over there, I still could not figure out the entire university by myself. When we had exams, we used to go a day before the exam to figure out which room and which building we had exam. It was a mystery the first day when I went, and it still is a mystery now. And I was just too lazy to get up and explore the university when I could explore the entire country!

My university life was very, very exciting! Everything was new! I woke up early and took a shower, put on clean clothes, used deodorant, and carried a notebook. And for some weird reason, I took 3 pens with me. Just in case. It's stupid, but still. I lost them all within a week, though. Where do all these pens go, anyway? Into a black hole?

It is always fun, the first day of school. I still remember me doing this when it was my first day of school, at the beginning of every grade. I would drag my father to the nearest stationary store, and buy all new stationery and new shoes, a Swat Cats bag, and Pokemon stationary. Ah! Nostalgia!

So, here, I did the same thing. I just did not have my Pokemon stationary with me. I had butterflies in my stomach, and I took my new backpack and my new pack of chewing gum with me (Chewing gum helps with making friends. Trust me with this), a bottle of coke and started out. This is how Hrithik Roshan enters every university in all the Bollywood films. A chewing gum and coke equals instant coolness.

The place where I was staying was a little away from the university, so we had to take the bus and then tram. I wanted to look trendy and fashionable, because first impressions count, and I hoped that some girl would at least look at me. Girls did look at me, but for entirely different reason. Let us not go there now.

I rushed to the Bus stop and was talking on the phone to another Indian friend, just to impress nearby girls on a bus stop, I shifted my conversation in English and to American accent which I learned from Hollywood movies. I quickly said bye to my friend (typical Indian behavior with friends). Now target was that beautiful girl. She was wearing black jeans with a light yellow scarf. She had blue eyes and was wearing Rayban brown glasses.

*I said "Hiii" to her,*

*She replied in a pleasant way "Helloo".*

*I asked her "Are you new in University?" The intention was just to contact her and talk.*

*She said, "Yes, I came last week".*

*I asked "in which course".*

*She replied "Botany".*

*I was ready for another question and apparently made a plan to impress her before the Bus came.*

*I quickly asked, "Are you from Germany?"*

*She said "No, I am from the US", then came to the heartbreaking sentence "You must be from India, you have Indian accent".*

I was shattered with her comment and my project to impress her with an American accent quickly failed.

OMG! Why its me again! Unlucky!

There was no further plan, I dropped the idea to impress her and waited for the Bus. From that day, I didn't want to show off. Finally, the Bus came and we sat on the different seat.

After that I had to take the metro to University, I observed that the entire compartment was filled with students, had a feeling of Mumbai fully loaded local train and as soon as the stop for the university came, the whole train, which just a few minutes ago was piled with people, got entirely empty. People vanished off the train as fast as Vada Pavs vanish in Mumbai or Bretzel from Schwabenland.

This wasn't just it! Every two minutes, there was a new train that would walk into the station, and hundreds of student would get out of it, and the empty train would go out of the station. Everybody had these backpacks with laptops in them, and earphones plugged in, so it looked like I was seeing the same person a thousand different times.

This university had close to 40,000 students studying there. Also, it has several departments with numerous lecturers. So, the lecturers, along with the students, and the helping staff, everybody was traveling in trains, so imagine the crowd that was coming out of the station. But, being from India, I was used to such crowds.

Students had an induction hour on that day, and it was supposed to start at 10:00 in the morning, so I thought I would be there at the university a little early, at least on the first day. A group of my friends and I entered the university and I was immediately mesmerized by its sheer size! It was so big! The campus was enormous! It could fit a hundred of my houses in it comfortably! In first look, it gazes like a big puzzle!

The induction was about to start, but we did not know where this hall was. We were searching and searching, but could not find the right room. We were as confused an Arts student in a Math class! We kept asking all the students, and finally one of them told us the correct directions. We were on the verge of getting late for the induction day, and so we asked this girl how far this lecture hall was. She very casually told us that it would take us around 20 minutes by walk. Something in the depth of my heart stopped when she said that. 20 minutes? We did not have that much of time! We told her that, and she suggested taking a bus. A bus! Inside the university!

Yes, university has special buses that run in the campus so that they can drop the students from one building to the other. We found one of the shuttle buses, and got on with it. And we reached that building which housed the lecture hall within minutes. We located the venue, and entered the vast room. The hall could accommodate more than 200 students. I suddenly remembered the scene from the film Munna Bhai, where they show massive auditorium kind of room that had semi-circle seating arrangements. The only difference was that the hall in which we entered was much bigger than the one in the movie. The whole place was just too big and looked plush. My friends and I entered, and took out seats together as a litter of puppies. We saw that the Head of our course was there to deliver the first lecture, and he had to talk into a mike to reach out to those sitting farther away from the dais.

We were warmly welcomed, and they told us all about the history of the university, and briefed us about the rules and regulations. We had an introduction with all of our Professors who would be teaching us. All of these Professors looked intellectual and learned. And I hate saying this, but I started feeling intimidated by them as soon as I saw them.

They gave us their cards, and we saw that not all of them were to be addressed as Professor; they all had more than one PhD, and were excellent in their respective fields. When we saw their cards, we noticed that all of their qualifications that they had mentioned there had taken up more than 70% of space on their card! We tried to talk to them, and they seemed interesting in knowing about our whereabouts and us. Being in the presence of all the people, makes my fluency in English even bad, and then I started stammering like an idiot in front of them. That time I didn't want to make the same mistake which I did in morning, so I used my usual English accent.

Professors were busy asking about our country, and as soon as they found out that I am from India, they launched into this questionnaire about the kind of life I lead there, and my education and my culture.

Our classes commenced after that, but I was so enticed with the sheer size of the classroom that I did not pay any attention to what my Professors were saying. But from the moment that I sat down in the class, I was so busy noticing all the new things around me that I completely forgot about the lecture that was going on! I heard the first one hour of the lecture, but after that, I was completely zoned out! It was partly because everything around me was too exciting for me to concentrate on the lecture that was going on.

The professors there are very tech savvy. They were even dressed well. I was sure that all the girls in my class were looking at them, and would never look at me. And the approach that they have toward teaching is entirely different from the way the lecturers in India teach. Everything over there was digital! We had projectors, and the professors there played slides and explained everything. And we did not even have to carry any notes or note down things like nerds. Damn! I was sad. I had just bought three pens for the notes! We could get the notes online and follow them up. This made me feel sad. It was so different from India, where the lecturer would come into the class with heavy books and guides and would jot down stuff on the blackboard, and we had to do the same thing too. In Germany, there were no notebooks, no guides, and no Xerox drama at the end of the semester. There were digital directories for us to go through as well.

This difference was fascinating to see, and even more exciting to experience. The quality of education over there was splendid, and I could see that they had invested a lot into making everything world class. Being a guy, and being a music fan, I did not fail to notice that even the speakers that they were using in the classrooms were from BOSE.

All these small memories are inked in my heart and I keep on remembering with my co-students. New challenges were waiting for us - Examinations and Project work.

Let me share a nice quote on colleges and universities by Mr.Hendren, that perfectly fits to my experience.

*"Parents send their kids to university either because they went to university or they didn't."*

# 5.  EXAMINATIONS

*Fear factor!*

My family hails from a tiny city, and all my life, my entire family had lived and survived in this city. So, for someone like me who had been born and brought up in a place where we had to struggle to have internet connections, this was a colossal deal. Even though the approach towards education was different, I think in a way this was convenient too. Maybe studying from laptops will motivate me to study more. But, that remains to be seen. For then, I would just have to get used to all of those tech-savvy education systems.

After we were done with the classes, all the Indian students who were studying at the University gathered together. In Germany, we were only "Indians", but back home, a South-Indian is a Madrasi, a guy from Gujarat is a business Gujju, a person from West Bengal is a Bong, North Indians are Bihari or Punjabi. Who even comes up with these names!? Innovative, aren't they?

So, all the people who had joined the university that semester had joined to discuss "Studies". Basically, it was just a lot of people who had gathered to figure out how they are going to cheat and pass the exams that we were supposed to face in coming future. We thought that we, being the smart asses that we were, would figure something out. Our seniors who had been at the university for quite a long time now, warned us and told us that nothing of that sort would be possible, but I did not listen to them. I did not listen to my 200-pound seniors back at my home, so, why on this great earth would I listen to somebody who was studying in Germany? So, off we went to discuss our notorious plans for the upcoming obstacles.

Now, all these cheating techniques are something like a loop. No matter how much you try, you will never come up with better methods. You will end up with the same old, tried and tested methods, and most often than not, these are of no use. But, will all that stop us from doing any of these things? Nope - Never. Even if we know that it is going to fail, and it is going to fail in a BIG way, we will never give up, and study for the exams. That just runs in our blood.

We thought of the usual transparent pens method, and we thought that we will somehow take our own papers from home, and will already have answers written on them. Another cool plan – in Germany we have a great benefit, which might seem lousy to others – one can wear thick and long jackets throughout the year, and I am sure that it will not look out of place. That is how cold it is over there! So, we could even stuff our thick furry jackets with these chits! I remember this one time when a guy from my college especially got a jacket made from a tailor in his neighborhood. This funky jacket had a faux lining underneath, just so that he could hide his notes there. Talk about going to lengths to pass one damn exam.

And of course, Toilets. How can I forget about Toilets? The official and traditional cheating spots since generations.

Dr.G

Actually, at that time, I might think that toilets are an excellent excuse and this idea is innovative as hell! But, later on, I found out that even people from my grandfather's generation would do the same thing. As I mentioned, it is a loop.

*We came with so many strategies. Even the United States probably did not come up with so many strategies when it wanted to invade Iraq.*

The exams were approaching. Exams are always approaching. I don't understand how this is possible. They are omnipresent! We were all self-assured of the fact that we would pass the exams, not matter what or how, because we had devised strategies for the toughest of the situations. If not Plan A, then we had Plan B and also Plan C. All the students were united, and I was so happy that this would work out.

So, finally came the day when our lecturers had to brief us about the upcoming exams. And when he told us about the exam, another SHOCK was waiting to hammer me. I was again shell shocked. I was so surprised that I did not know how to react. At first, I actually thought that my Professor was kidding, and was playing some kind of a prank. I could never understand the humor of these German people! It is arid. But, he was not. He told us that it was going to be an open-book exam.

*What is an Open-Book Exam?*

It means that we could bring all the material, books, guides, chits, and notes in the examination hall. To the examination hall! We could officially see and write. Copying and pasting never sounded so good in my life.

I was awed! We could get whatever we want. That seems incredibly easy! No need for any Plan!

There must be some sort of a catch somewhere. Why in the whole world would they teach us the entire semester, with loads of power point presentations, guest lectures, and a sizable amount of notes and all if we just had to research from some books in the exam hall and fill in our answer sheets. I thought that there would be too many questions for us to answer. But, this was not the catch too. We only had to answer four questions. Four! This had to be easy. Or, it was what we thought.

Our professors told us that they did not actually bother about the final answer that we would be getting in the exam. That was not even one of their concerns. They wanted to see our "approach" towards the problem or question. And so, we were given all the freedom. We could go to the library and take whichever book that we needed for the exam, and there would be no need to study.

I felt this was a sweet SHOCK, it was surprising but I loved it. No need to learn anything. I was already in love with Germany. Imagine a lecturer in India telling you that you could copy and pass the exam. The mere thought of it makes me laugh.

We all came out of the lecture halls and gathered together and laughed so much about the whole thing. So much of planning went into us thinking about how we would take the small bits of papers and notes inside the classroom, and here, the lecturers themselves were asking us to get whatever we wanted to. This has to be the best thing ever. All of the coats with the faux lining were going to be a waste.

The German intelligence is nothing compared to our super grand strategies. But we understood. By then, all the seniors in the university had become good friends of ours, so we went to them for advice. Turned out, that the professors can do whatever they want.

These open book exams are notorious things of the highest degree! It breaks friendships in a matter of seconds. All of the group strategies that we had thought of until now were abandoned abruptly. Now, it was all a one-man army. All the people who had planned things together suddenly started studying and we could see a lot of "Do Not Disturb" boards in the corridors of the dormitory. All the books on that particular subject just vanished off the shelves of the library in just two days. I went to check out the books from the library after a day, and had to come back home empty handed. Well, not really empty handed, I bought along a few comics and magazines. But, none of the study material that I actually required. Everyone was seriously studying. But the thing is, even if we had like a thousand reference books to read, how would we even finish them before the exam? We did not know anything of this sort. That was the first time in our life we heard the term "open book exam"!

We went to the assistant of our professor, thinking that he would help us with this. We thought that with some puppy-eyed faces, we could somehow gain his sympathy, and know the questions. He was a German guy, and he did not help us in any way. He just told us how the whole thing works. We came to the university thinking that we would play some kind of a team game like, well, cricket

(My love for this game never ends). However, turned out that we were going to be all alone like in a marathon, after all!

Also, I have got a confession to make. Since there was not any kind of an attendance procedure there, I had bunked a lot. There was never a particular time for a single class, so I kept missing many classes, and that would affect me then. Who could have foreseen this? I was just enjoying my freedom!

The day of the exam came, I took my lucky glasses. Thank God, I bought good number of eye wear or specs, as I checked they are dam expensive in Germany. As per weight of eyeglasses and frames, they are expensive than gold. It is because of brand name. We were told that we could sit where ever we wanted to. We could not even copy if we wanted to, because it would be very evident if our approach towards the questions were similar. The brilliant professors would figure things out within minutes. So, I set out to answer the questions myself.

The questions were very practical. There was nothing twisted about them, and they all had a very logical answer, I am sure. My whole time went off in just trying to understand the wordings of the questions! Now, answering them was the next step. I read the first one, and it seemed easy enough. So, I set out to answer that. After that, answering the remaining was like a nightmare.

Finally, when I had come out of the exam hall, I had attempted two questions out of the four. I knew that I was going to fail. But till, when everyone came out of the exam hall, they burst out laughing! I didn't understand why people were laughing when they come out of an exam! Maybe it's a universal thing. But, I was just happy that it was over!

*A journey of a thousand miles begins with a single step.*

After writing two exams, we clearly understood that if we wish to pass the exam there, we had to study and that should be done in an analytical approach. The strategies of rote memory and copying that we used to apply towards exams in India cannot be applied here, that one fact was crystal clear to all us. It was a classic case of Do or Die. So I quickly started for next steps. I realized quickly that only hard work and continuous study could help me out. These small steps helped a lot to build a strong base. In the end, I used to study continuously for more than 50 hours without a single nap!

# 6. MAKING OF "MADE IN GERMANY"

*Oh God, help me!*

*"There is no substitute for hard work."*

A well-known and common quote said by Thomas A. Edison. But that hard work of continuous study was not enough to get "MADE IN GERMANY" tag.

I really didn't know that many more surprises were waiting for us. However we realized that the courses were quite interesting. And when we seriously sat down to study we found that it was interesting and that we were doing some kind of technical stuff.

It was amazing because that was the first time we had come across such a type of education system. However, it was challenging because it kindled and forced our thoughts and ideas to be brought out in the open. In the initial stages, we all boast that we would design multiple story buildings, cars, rockets and all sorts of things moreover we planned to beat the esteemed AMGs or Chhabria designs as soon as we step out of college. German university was in all terms making us equipped with particular skills which would enable us to build things from a paper boat to IT parks to Rockets, all with our own hands and our own minds.

In the second semester, we clearly understood the professor's expectations and that was to be practical and original. We had already seen that they didn't force or expect us to learn the theory part and feed it in our brains. It took time for our brains to realize that it was no tomfoolery and we had to accept it and we had Hobson's choice. Thus, we steered towards German system of education from Indian system of education, all for our sake.

Then it was the last semester and we had 'Project Work or Master Thesis' to get this world famous the stamp on us. It was very interesting part of my journey. I say interesting because I didn't know that it would blow our minds off later. In Germany, project work is teamwork where we have to form a group of four and do it. We meticulously followed the same measures and procedures, which we did in previous studies. Search, copy, edit and paste from the Internet, Book, magazine. That was exactly how we did our project and hoping that it would at least let us pass if not the best. We were very confident and trusted the work that we had done.

After three weeks we received our evaluated project. In my whole life, I had never seen a feedback of such a type and size. Our project report came completely RED with feedbacks!

Before, we started reading the feedback from the professor the red marked one, we all were thinking could it be possible that someone is trying to play prank on us.

The funniest part was that, before getting Professor's Feedback, we all were betting who will get the best score. I was expecting to get Excellent. Grow up Boys, after seeing such feedback, it was a new challenge to pass. Forget about the excellent score.

That was the first time I beheld such an enormous feedback. The professor's feedback was more in volume than what I had written in my report. I had written some 70 pages and the professor's feedback was as if it ran for more than that. In India, feedback by professor in such detail would be a rarity. When I received my book, I was sure that the book was thoroughly read by the professor and the professor himself had turned red with anger rushing to his cheeks.

It was a completely handwritten feedback, which seemed as if the professor was praising us, though it was nothing less than the abuses. Experience was new for both, we the students as well as for the professor who had never seen such a report from intelligent and skilled students, as we would like to call ourselves nor we were expecting such a detailed analysis of our work. We had not cited the sources from where we had copied and pasted the work, whether it was from Wikipedia or from some other website.

Our project concept was unique but not the text. How to give a reference, how to use text, how to use photo etc., for all these things professor recommended us some additional books. More books and then again more books ....

*GOD HELP ME !*

*God promptly replied ... I CAN'T ...... Do it Yourself!*

The pictures that we had pasted were also not the right ones and the pixels were not right, which made the pictures unclear and was sure to bring a frown on anybody's face but only we didn't notice it. The text itself was not enough. The conclusion was also a blunder. There were many tips from Professor. To improve that Professor recommended us other student's thesis.

We did not have any guts to meet the professor personally. Therefore, we asked his assistant about it. That was another mistake, which we committed. Another session of more than an hour, where we received our personal feedbacks, that was further more embarrassing.

Like the professor, he was also surprised to see that intelligent fellows like us worked so badly on a project. I didn't understand where I had gone wrong though I knew it already that didn't seem a matter to be blown up so big. Being young and energetic we didn't accept our mistake. I was focusing only on the idea and professors were teaching us the whole development process. Then I realized the significance of the words "MADE IN GERMANY". It didn't seem just a small tag anymore. Those people who are "MADE IN GERMANY" are actually perfectionists, a perfectionist like Aamir Khan or Serena Williams.

The professor didn't accept to see our presentation, because he first wanted to read the thesis. He religiously wanted to read the thesis book then proofread it and then he would show the green signal for us to make our presentation. My mind raced back to the examinations and questioned me- were the exams tough or the project work? I could answer it. The project report was the toughest one.

After listing motivation songs and reading about other failures, and most important after watching mud bike race where the racer falls many times in mud, but still make a stand and run and to surprise he sometimes wins the race. For me it was likewise to finish the race after my falls - sorry in my case thesis not race.

The young and energetic Indian in me gave way to lateral thinking. I suddenly felt wisdom seep into me from all sides. I was optimistic. It is from our mistakes that we learn. We immediately rolled up our sleeves and plunged into the process of editing our projects. It wasn't editing though, it was writing. Because we had only copied and pasted the entire content. The professor had clearly warned us that he would not accept such kind of low-quality reports. He needed the reports of the best quality. We started to prepare ourselves for the German tag. It took days for us, each day and night, we worked hard to meet the criteria.

The best quality and finally at the end of one full month we submitted the report. The report was now not like what it was before. We tried to transform our Indian Bull-Cart to a German made Car. It was thoroughly renovated into a piece of writing which an expert would do. Now I was in full confidence that the report would do wonders and was confident about my marks as well. This time my confidence came from my hard work, unlike earlier.

Finally received the tag- "MADE IN GERMANY". Indeed, it has meaning.

There were many ups and downs in our lives. We had to undergo a lot of pressure. However, it was all part of phase of learning. That phase turned me into a mature and capable young man. It was our sheer luck that we got a part-time job in the university itself. University life has many facets. Moreover, it is tough for everyone to combine all those incidents and put them into a single chapter. A person has to experience this life to totally understand it in all terms.

*This helps me also to understand this idiom ....*

*"God helps those who help themselves"*

# 7.  HOSTEL

*Where Sherlock Holmes fails!*

Hostels have a magic of their own and the feeling of living in a hostel is different. Every person should experience this at least once in a lifetime. It's about living alone, getting independent, washing dishes, clothes and to locate things without mother. Living in a hostel had taught me many valuable lessons, and had helped me adjust later in my life.

I was staying in the university hostel and they did not have a separate hostel for girls and boys. Yes, it's right. Hostels are common for both guys and girls, and when I found that out, my brain mentally started doing a tap dance. My neighbor can be a girl wearing hot clothes, and roaming around me all days and nights, or it can be a hairy guy from Australia who drinks and yells every night.

I was, of course, hoping that it would be girls who would be my neighbors, and I was anticipating the wait till the lists of the hostels were put up by the administration. I wished that I had gone to the gym right before coming here, but instead, I stuffed my face with food that was deep-fried and loads of homemade stuff. So, imagine how I was looking,

Students from different cultures and from every part of the world, and for the next few years, they were my neighbors. While the hostels were huge with wide corridors, there was no sharing room concept. The university hostels are usually the preferred choice for the international students, as most of them are not familiar with the city, and they would rather live in the vicinity of the college. Though, most of the local students prefer to live outside the college in rented apartments, international students lived in those hostels.

We had no mess or canteen to provide food for us, which was actually a blessing in disguise for us, as I could have never been able to digest the food there. Moreover, they could not apparently cook for the students who were there from half the world in there. Imagine, if a Japanese guy wanted to eat snails for lunch. Therefore, we were allotted shared kitchens and we had to share with around 4 to 5 others students. We could cook whatever we wanted over there, and we all used to cook separately. I rather liked it that way, as I thought that we could bond over food!

During the weekend, when everyone was lying around in the hostel and had to cook the lunch, the stink that used to emanate from all the vegetable and the fish and the raw meat and all the other ingredients in the kitchen was something more than hell. It was like living in a dump yard, with corridors and beds all around. There were Koreans, French, and Japanese and Chinese people all around me, and everyone used to try their hand at the food and I had to stand there, holding on to my breath and taking in all the flavors of the world, quite literally. How can the smell of food be bad? When we go to a restaurant, with smell of the food within seconds our mouth starts watering and we drool like 2-year-olds because the food is from a single cuisine. However, my hostel was a different case, no proper ventilation, and we had 5 people cooking 5 different things.

Nevertheless, the good thing about having so many people from different cultures around, was that I could always taste all of their food, and I used to eat almost everything that was cooked there. This was my way of knowing a person, and being an Indian, I would totally form judgments and create opinions about the person based on their food. None of them was great cook, but it was like going to a restaurant and trying out various cuisines. It was my free buffet, and I could never go hungry there. In the evenings, after the classes were done, we would all sit together and share our food, and this was such a pleasant feeling! It was unbelievable fun there!

We had a common fridge in the hostel room, and everyone used to keep their stuff over there in the refrigerator. I love flavored yogurt, and I just used to dump huge packs of these when I was in college. I ate them like popcorn all the time. So, once I had bought around 4 packs of them, and the next time I opened the fridge, I found 2 of them missing. I, absent-minded genius, thought that I might have gulped them down in night. But, the next time, the same thing was repeated, and I realized that some of my yogurts were missing. This was not usual. I bought a kilo of grapes and they were stolen too, the scenario kept going on for a while.

*What the hell?*

Stealing in the hostel is not only in India, but students are same everywhere. Five others used to live with me in the same apartment, and I did not know whom to suspect. I had put up notices and stuck up sticky notes, but of no use. Then another of my roomy said that his food was also getting stolen. Suddenly, everybody's food was disappearing and we were clueless about- what to do? Frequency paced up, It was evident that somebody among us was the culprit and was doing it deliberately, as nobody could come from outside at night, all the doors were closed, and honestly, who would come and take all the risk to just steal a kilo of grapes!

Now I hit upon a plan! A brilliant ingenious plan and my detective instincts started ushering out of me. I wanted to catch the culprit who did this and was ready to go to any length to finish him off. I took that red-chilli powder that my mom had packed in huge boxes and I mixed it with a little water. Then, I took this water and infused it into the yogurt with the help of a little straw. I made a tiny hole in the pack, and with the aid of a thin straw, I somehow infused the yogurt with some of the chili water.

I tried to be the detective genius, Sherlock Holmes, and I thought that the person who would eats this will either end up in the bathroom due to the spiced up version of my yogurt. They were all foreigners, and I knew how these people react to the spicy food of Indian. I was so confident of catching the prick, who was indulging in thefts that I did not think for once that my plan might fail. I kept my designed trap in the fridge and waited for it to be stolen, which I was sure would happen eventually. I waited and waited. One day passed by and my yogurt was still there. Then, another day passed, and my yogurt was still there. I started panicking. I thought that maybe this thief had figured out my plan, or must have found out somehow, that is why he hadn't stolen anything till then. Still, I left the yogurt to be there. I waited patiently, and on the third day, that person finally took the yogurt. Aha! As planned, Sherlock never fails.

Now I started waiting for that cry of pain from this guy. Or, at least, his face should turn red. But, guess what? There was nothing. That guy happily ate the yogurt and left no clue behind him, and I was left with nothing at all. I wanted to show off in front of my friends, and it failed big time. As usual!

So, after my master plan failed me, we went to our old ways- Not to store the food, buy and eat the food on the same day. We even thought to install a webcam in the room, but we were so broke, I could not even buy any more yogurt packs, let alone pay for a webcam. And so, this thief story ended with failing of Sherlock and my plan.

Lots of stories filled my entire college life. Every Thursday evening, there used to be a party that was hosted by the students of the university itself, and this was the kind of stuff that I was waiting for. These parties were just like the parties that they would see in the Hollywood movies, and every week, we would expect these parties to start. We could see pretty girls from the other buildings, loud music, alcohol and everyone used to be on the dance floor till late in the night. These parties we honestly fun, and we went there to relax after a week of hectic schedules and mind-boggling classes.

There was another funny incident that had happened to me during my stay in the hostel, and I still remember this incident vividly! 1st April or April fool day is not so famous in Germany but in the hostel it is. Everybody used to have one or the other pranks up their sleeve, and they were just looking for an opportunity to go prank somebody.

Among my roommates, we had a Korean guy who used to live in the room adjacent to mine. This guy was pure fun, and we used to have a lot of pranks and jokes going around when he was around. He was a hedonist and was always up to something or the other, so we even were wary when he was around because you might just be his next victim.

This Korean guy had a girlfriend who was in our university as well, and she used to live in the next hostel. But, on almost all the days, she would just crash in our room at his place, and they both made an excellent pair too, as even the girl was a very mischievous one, and would prank all the other people along with this guy.

They both used to have a lot of fun together, and it was exciting to hang out with them all the time.

So, on this one day that was April Fool's day, it was about 11:00 PM and we all were sleeping, and I could hear this couple in the next room. Everybody had gone to sleep, and I was awake in my room. Suddenly, I could hear some moans and sounds coming out from their room. And it started getting louder and louder. At first, I thought that it is just of their voices, talking.

But, oh my god! I realized what they were later on! They were having sex and wild way.

I could hear their voices from across the damn thin wall. The girl was moaning, and it started getting louder and louder with each minute. I freaked out. I cannot tell how strange the feeling is to just sit there and hear wild roommate. I came out of the room and slowly, all the other people in the adjacent rooms started coming out hearing their voices. They were all uncomfortable, and we were sitting in the kitchen not knowing what to do. We kept giving each other uncomfortable glances because we could not do anything. The main door was already close for the night, and we were just stuck there in that room with that couple having sex in the room next to ours. How I was praying that they would stop, and it would be sunrise soon.

Suddenly, I could sense that the voices seemed to be moving closer to us.

*Now much closer !*

Our eyes popped out, both came to the kitchen door and indeed with wild loudness. Both were semi-naked and had a music system with them. They just played the loud sex voice in music system.

*YAAAA! Only music system.*

He yelled APRIL FOOLS loudly!!

I though it's weird prank. But no, not at all. All of us started laughing and we could not stop for hours and hours together! We were so stunned! And, relieved at the same time. After that we had a long night after party. The Korean couple was the star of that night.

*Waaw, what a prank!*

# 8.  GRIFTER GIRL

*Live with drifter and grifter*

$F$inally, it happened!! I got my dream job in the most famous automobile company, which I had been eyeing for a long. The company was located in a different city, and this city was bigger than the present city that I was living in. I learned so much over here, and I was hungry to learn more.

Since this job was in another city, I had to move to the city in few months. House hunting in Germany is as easy as fighting for free food in India, which means, one might die in the process, but will not achieve it.

I asked my friends who were in that city to help me out, but that also did not work out. Friends gave free advice to search new job in another city. It's easy to get job but not an apartment. It was just a few days before until I had to move to a new city and I tried approaching that problem by approaching brokers. However, that didn't work out too as they asked me fee, which was more than my three months rent of any flat and unknown to them my financial condition was such that I was, thinking how I was going to pay the rent for three months. Moreover, for Pete's sake, why would I just pay that much? This option was also gone.

Nevertheless, after begging people from here and there, and contacting people somehow, one of my friend suggested that I should check if there are any apartments in that area, which are being sub-let. By Sub-let, he meant that I should check if there was any person who was going to another country for a while in some business and that was what exactly I wanted, at least to have a temporary apartment.

Luckily, I found one such apartment for myself. I checked out the area and found that the place was feasible for me moreover it was located right near the place where I was supposed to work. It was a girl, who was sub-letting the apartment to be précised a beautiful Girl

I e-mailed that girl right away saying that I need that place as soon as possible, and I got a reply from her saying that apartment had all the facilities like a refrigerator, a washing machine, internet connection and also with a kitchen. My happiness knew no boundaries, it was like icing on the cake, a cheap fully furnished apartment. What an achievement. The girl further informed that she was subletting the apartment as she was going on a 3 months' vacation and her purpose behind subletting the house was that there would be someone to look after it while she was away.

I asked the girl to send me some photographs of that apartment just to have an idea of what it looks like, and she e-mailed me some pictures of her apartment. I could see a big room, some furniture, a huge kitchen all was decently done. Although I could see that there were some really, girly things that were lying around the house those were all in a very violent shade of pink. But, I thought I can adjust with it for a while. A metrosexual man likes pink anyway, and I thought that I could teach myself to embrace that.

After a while, I gave her a call and asked few questions. She astonished me with her voice and the way of talking. Indeed, I forgot all the points what I wanted to clarify. Most important was to reduce the rent but forget about reducing she told me that I had to pay more for electricity heating etc. Though I wanted to say It was not mentioned in the advertisement, I end up saying of course I would bear the electricity and heating bill. I felt hypnotized by her voice.

After the call, I analyzed that she is too good in management. I have to learn from her and have to meet her soon. I told the girl that I would be arriving over there in two weeks, and that I would be taking that place. But, the girl said that she would be leaving the city the next week itself.

*What ? (All my plans collapsed, I was upset not because my plans collapsed but why so quickly)*

She was looking at somebody who could moves in as soon as possible. I thought that I would never be able to find a deal that was as good as this, and I jumped at this opportunity like a bunny that has been giving a bundle of carrots. I knew carrots were not weed as what I was expecting however, I needed an apartment. So, I told her to reserve that apartment for me. She told me that if I wanted her to reserve the apartment for me, then I should wire her the money within the week. I had to send the money to her account, including the rent for the first month and the security deposit.

I thought though I had never seen the apartment myself, but the photos looked good enough and when she can live there, why not me?

Thinking this, I agreed to do so, and told the girl that I would send her the money for the room in a week's time. Honestly, I was not sure of that. Nevertheless, I had no other choice so I sent the money to her next week. Since I had never met the girl I tried to check her profiles and other details on the social media, and she seemed fine. I was sure that it was not a fake profile, and that genuinely was a girl. So, finally, the day came when I had to travel to another city to start my internship, and I took a bag with me and some luggage and took a train to the other city.

As the journey was long and I was exhausted not because of travelling but because of packing my stuffs. I went to that apartment and I found the correct address, and as I had seen some photos of the apartment, I could recognize it, and I went ahead into the building and knocked on the door.

I was sure that she must have left but still praying if she missed her flight or she is ill and at home. Daydreaming! I knocked again! No answer. I knocked again. And again, nobody opened it. I rang the bell and waited, and waited for some more time. She had promised that she would give the keys of her apartment to the neighbor and would tell him that I would be coming. So, I approached the neighbors and thought I will just take the keys of my "new" apartment from them.

There was a Turkish restaurant next door, and I went over to ask them about the apartment. I was also happy to be next to that restaurant as I can smell the delicious food and don't have to go a long way to find fast food. I asked him that I am about to sublet the apartment next door, and I asked him for the keys. I met the blank look. I understood he might don't know German. So, I switched to English and greet him by "Salam" and again he gave me a weird look. He replied me in perfect German "Was willst du? What you want?

Thank God! He replied and I asked him about keys. I told him again, and he just smirked at me and told me that there is no apartment here, and that place that I was looking at was just a parking house!

I was sure he didn't understand what I was asking him and I showed him it's not left side I mean right side apartment and requested him to come and see the apartment I am asking about.

He promptly said, "I know what you are asking, you are not the only one!" As soon as he said that, something inside my stomach did a back flip and I suddenly got that clenching feeling. I thought, and hoped, that I had somehow ended up on the wrong street, and that the place I was looking at was the wrong one. I checked and re-checked the number of the street, and the house number, and I could see that everything was correct.

I went to the Turkish guy again and showed him my contract and told him that I was planning on subletting that apartment and that I had paid the money for it already. He also checked and rechecked the contract, and he told me that I was not on the wrong street, but just that there was no apartment there. It was just a multi-level kind of a parking lot, and people just keep their old vehicles over there. The only way I could live there was if

I could kip under rotting old cars. This was when I started flipping out. I had no internet then, and so I called up my friend to ask him to check the internet. We checked on Google Street View, and over there, my friend saw that it indeed was some kind of a warehouse, but it was hidden in the street view.

I went to the coffee shop next door, and he told me that the contract that I was holding in my hand was a fake one! I was shocked! I was cheated!

The owners and all the people around told me that I was not the only one who had come to that place with a contract in their hand. Infact, there were several other people who had come with similar contracts and said that they were subletting the same apartment. These people, whoever they were, were cheating a lot of people, and I sadly was one of their victims. I immediately called up the police. I wanted to take some action and hand these people to the police. The police arrived and they took my statement and told me the same thing that I was not the only one who had fallen into the trap, and they had already received many other complaints before mine. The account that I had wired the money to was some foreign country's account, so there was no easy way that I could get my money back.

I did not know what to do. I just looked up for some hostels in the nearby places, and found one, and while I was doing my Job, I stayed at the hostel. It was so expensive! However, I had to do this.

*After this episode, I learned my lesson! Never trust anybody blindly!*

# 9. DRIVING

*Zebra is the Cobra!*

Next phase of life started after I married my school time girlfriend. After our marriage, she joined me in Germany and this journey shifted from my cultural shocks to our cultural shocks.

We were totally impressed with scenic charisma of Germany and seamless road experience. Germany is famous for its luxurious and high performance cars. Being creator of Automotive, Germany has a history of 130 years of automotive development and still at the top place. It is because of its car and speed lover.

Autobahn is the federal highway system in Germany with no toll tax and no speed limit.

*IMAGINE ...... NO SPEED LIMIT!*

Germany offers to drive at 300 km/hour of speed and hence, wider roads for appropriate utilization of the car's assets. The sign boards itself say one can drive with as much speed as one wants. Isn't it amazing! All the "fast and furious" things can be tried as many times one want, which is otherwise not possible in a country like India. Although India is known for its unity in diversity, the rule is not applicable to the Indian roads.

It has been a while in Germany I gained the competence to manage my path by all the German means. No doubt, this process involves churning down my Indian state of mind, but the result is me becoming a prudent par excellence.

To enjoy this factor, one has to pass an authoritarian driving exam with zero tolerance. Theory as well as practical is a big challenge if one sticks to the Indian way of driving. For me, I quickly shifted my Indian way to German way and passed both exams in one go. Other Indian friends were shocked when they came to know that I passed the exam in one go. I have a magical tip, which helped me as well as others to pass the driving practical exam.

Intercultural Guru Dr.G's has a magical advice to clear the practical exam and it is while taking the practical exam thinks and behaves like a retired old person in 60s. Let pass other vehicle if they have priority, don't rush and don't show sporty driving skills. Be calm, patience and follow only the rules.

Now the time was to experience the driving. Being a traditional Indian who was forced to press brake more than the race for almost all the time, driving a car on the autobahn was indeed a blessing. Another Indian way of driving was to put one hand on steering and one hand on the hand. It doesn't work in Germany. Honking meant to warn or abuse someone. When I was visiting the highway, I drove my car with standard Indian speed of 80 km/hr. However, when I saw people overhauling me, I accelerated my car and was immersed in the mystified beauty of the highway. Here, speed thrills not kills!

Though highway offers no speed limit, but in the urban areas the speed is limited to 50 km/hr. There are mandated limits for accident prone, under construction, substandard and urban areas. German federal law is very particular about human safety and traffic rules. That's why every car requires TÜV certificate to drive and it is valid only for two years.

Once, I decided to rent a convertible car for a weekend. The plan was to go for a long drive to Alps regions. The day started with 20°C and reached 35 until midday, it was really hot, and we were not able to enjoy in the open car. Therefore, we decided to take a break in a nearby town and have local food, restaurants in small town and villages are awesome. Ask the locals and go for it. We did the same and before reaching to the restaurant, we saw there was a traffic jam and people were loud. It is unusual so I came out and saw that some Indians were trying to cross the road on Zebra crossing. Indians were waiting before Zebra crossing and car drivers were telling them in German to cross. People were loud and saying *"are you drunk!"*, *"Weirdo!"*, *"Go learn some rules!"* in German to that Indians.

I quickly went there and told them to cross the road. By law, pedestrians have priority to cross the road if there is Zebra crossing. I remembered my initial days, being from India it never happened that any car driver gives priority to pedestrians, no matter if there is Zebra or Cobra. Even if I knew this rule, it is not easy to digest and take the risk to cross the road if the car is coming towards me.

I told them this rule, irrespective of the signal, if one finds pedestrian along the Zebra crossing, vehicle has to stop to let the pedestrian cross it first. No matter how much time it takes, one has an emergency or getting late for the office, it is mandatory to take care at Zebra crossing.

Zebra is like a cobra for drivers in Germany. If knowingly or unknowingly, the car touches the Zebra Crossing it bites back like a cobra and vehicle driver will definitely end up canceling the driving license or heavy fines or both.

*Here, big things are admired, but small things are loved the most!*

Furthermore, if a car meets with an accident major or minor one, the legitimate process is to call the Police at first. Police examine the car, informs the insurance company and only then, one can get the repair done for the damage. Not only this, the car with slightest of the scratch follows the same legitimate process. This is the reason Germany has scratch less cars on road. I know every country has its own rules and customs, but beforehand information about the same is vital.

Mercedes-Benz's "The Best or nothing", BMW's "Sheer Driving Pleasure", Audi's "Advancement through Technology" or Porsche's "there is no substitute" are not just tagline. They have true meaning and can be enjoyed to the most on German autobahns.

# 10.  MAFIA

*Mystery behind the Mystery Calls*

Mafia stories often come from renowned places like Italy and Dubai. But, I was surprised when I faced a Mafia attack in Germany - the place known for sophistication and geniality.

*No Kidding, I truly faced!*

Unlike other countries, Mafia in Germany attacks with no gun, no rifle but with papers. *Yes, it is true with PAPER.* It was a bad morning. I had already lost my one and only watch, was late for the office, and my wife was out of town. Preparing breakfast was not an issue, but I missed her secret ingredient and flavor in the food. After having my morning food, I always check my mailbox to find for letters and bills.

It is highly required because I visit a doctor for regular check-ups and in Germany the invoice, fee receipt and money statement for every consult comes through mail after two or more weeks of consultation. Privately insured persons receive these bills later on to pay. And, after receiving the bill, the money has to be transferred immediately to the respective account.

*Dr.G*

While I was asserting the mailbox, there I found a letter from an anonymous sender from North Germany. I furiously opened it to find what's hidden under it. The letter goes as—

*To Dr. G (to me),*

*Address,*

*From (anonymous sender, advocate)*

*Subject: Payment of 180 euros due*

*Dear Dr. G,*

*On the behalf of X laboratory, this is a legal statement of having you fined for not submitting your medical bill. You got your blood test done on (xx date) that is almost two years back and you were liable to pay twelve euros. It was back then, but now, you will have to pay twelve euros plus the interest rate of two years. Additional to that one hundred and fifty euros as my (advocate) fees of sending you the mail. Hence, your total comes as 180 euros.*

*You have missed the payment and the lab authorities want to case the file against you. I shall recommend you pay the amount by this week to avoid any further consequences or any 'otherwise'. We may drag you to the court and shall ensure that we present solid charge sheet against you. If you want a clean passage, kindly pay the money soon.*

*Kind regards,*

*XYZ*

*WTF !!! §$?&§$#%§&$ !!!*

*My reaction to this that letter.*

Then I thought, it must be a spam. However, to confirm it, I called on the attached number given in the letter. The ungracious voice picked up the phone. I inquired and said about what all was written in the letter. He said, "Yes it is true, and if you do not want us to increase the payment amount, send the payment sooner." I stressed upon the fact that I agree that I had missed it, and I will pay twelve euros plus the interest, but I won't be paying any other extra euro for your stupid hefty fee. He hanged upon me saying, "The sooner it is, the better it will be for you."

I knew something of this bad was going to happen, for my morning started within an incorrect tone first, I was missing my wife badly then I was not finding my clothes, shoes etc. "Why my wife put stuff in such a way that I cannot find! I am sure I am not the only one." I called her, asked for the stuff and narrated about that letter too. According to her, I am very watchful of bank and bill statements so, she said with an assurance that I can never miss such statement. She said, "The guy must be fooling you around. It can be a joke or a prank. Do not worry stay calm. Maybe some friend of yours is doing this". But I had already confirmed that, by call.

However, the letter and the phone conversation with the advocate kept me infuriated. Therefore, I decided to know more about that man. I searched on the Internet to find whether the advocate is genuine. I wanted to know about his previous cases and association with the laboratory. But, even Google did not know who the man was. It gave no relevant results. Then, believing what my wife assured me I ignored and assumed it a prank and left for the office. That whole incident already made me 2 hours late for the office.

After two days my wife returned, I hugged her to feel the warmth. I was relieved to much extent, not because of that letter but then I could find my stuff quickly. More than anything else, she was the source of motivation and encouragement for me. I always thank God for all the good and bad days we spent together.

How stupid I am! In such a difficult time, I am telling my love story.

Back to Mafia, the next morning was supposed to be the Good morning, as the breakfast had to come from my wife's kitchen. Nothing to miss anymore, I was so carried away by the fact of her being with me that I forget about that anonymous letter. The letter was then two days old. Everything was in order and I was happy. Then I checked my mailbox as it comes with my routine.

I was surprised to find another letter from the same source. It says—

*"... As you called me, used my valuable time which cost 40€, the money has been now increased to 220 euros. Every per minute conversation between us has been charged and added to the total. Within next three days' pay the bill or be ready to face other consequence...."*

*WTF !!! §§?&§$#%§&$%§§%§§&$%§&§'&§%§$ !!!*

*I had the similar reaction with longer extension to that newly received letter.*

In next weeks, the bill appeared regularly. The amount was increased to 400 euros, as I didn't pay the money. My eyes popped out. It was too much to take then. I called the advocate to fight over the phone for if that was some kind of prank then it was not working. I dialed the number and the same voice picked up. I said many things all together and busted him with the most arrogant words and phrases.

Then after a long pause I asked him, " why are you bothering me every now and then for no reason. It is useless to pay 400 euros for missed 12 euros for the lab report." He said, "Okay, it is your first time therefore, we give you a discount. Now you have to pay 200 euros in next two days." It was then I realized he was not an advocate but a Mafia asking for money otherwise. I asked for time to think.

I discussed with my friends and they approved of the recent call from the advocate and asked me to give away the amount. According to them, if I did not pay, he would take the case to court and then I would have to hire my personal advocate who would charge around 500-600 euro, which would be an additional burden. Therefore, it was better to give away the money and get back the calmness.

However, I disapproved the suggestion given by my friends. If I missed any payment, I would pay the net amount of 12 euros and the interest and not even a single penny more than that. I asked for the final verdict from my wife, as she is from a family of advocates, but in India.

How so ever all tacts and tricks of law, she carries in her blood. She suggested me not to waste much of my time and rush to the court and explain all to the authority to bring some sense to those letters.

For the first time, I visited the German court. The court was like a classic building, old architecture but modern interior. There was no advocate, no photocopy shops, no tea stall etc. I couldn't imagine such court. I literally asked them where the court was and they said that I was in a court. I felt as if it was my first day in school, I was enthusiastic, eager, nervous, anxious, and was staring at every board in the court.

I got one nice woman and I thought she was the manager or was on some senior post, as I was staring at every board. She asked me if she could help.

*I found the shoulder to cry.*

I explained everything right from mystery letters to the calls. One of the representatives assisted in bringing the situation down. He inquired at the laboratory if I missed on any of the bill payments. Unfortunately, I did miss the payment for 12 euros. She advised me there is no need to hire personal advocate in fact, I should script down the issue on paper and submit it to the honorable judge. My case would be studied and eventually the judge would issue the final verdict, himself. No intermediate lawyer is required for it. Finally, I decided to follow his instructions and as per the verdict I had to pay just 20 euros (12 euros plus interest) to the respective laboratory. Phew! The government authorities ultimately took off the situation.

Process was slow and same like in India, it had been three years from now and I didn't hear anything about it. Such a relief! Hope this relief continues.

The court administrator advised me to get an advocate Insurance, if in future I face such situation I shall be able to hire my own advocate. The insurance starts at the very nominal price. I strongly advise people living and working in Germany to get that insurance fasten than Mafia. And, beware of illegal and paper mafias!

*"Illegal is always faster." by Eoin Colfer*

# 11. LIVING CULTURE

*Save a Laughter, Tick Tock Your*
*Clock an Hour To or Fro*


Europe is unarguably appalled and praised for its scenic beauty, which is well, reflected when one witnesses it in the movie or on the larger platforms. In summers, Germany gives similar hues of Switzerland. Its panorama, feel, surrounding and fragrance always remind me of the land known for unique ecologies. Although, the climate conditions and weather is similar to India, their implication is different in Germany. German weather is not punctual like Germans. German winter can come much early and knock the door, not even the door it can knock the soul with -20°C freezing wind.

Being from engineering background and a boy, I am very bad in defining colors, unlike girls (I mean beautiful girls) who knows 100s of pink color shades. I would like to classify German seasons in colors - yellow, white and gray. Summer in Germany is pleasant with yellowish hue all around and temperature ranging not more than 35 degrees. As said, German weather is unlike German. Last few year summer reached 40°C too. True, 40°C in Germany, without Air condition and in summer it is a big challenge to find a fan to buy. Can you imagine snowfall in Bangalore or Delhi or in Chennai? Same way it is hard to imagine 40°C in Germany.

A welcoming winter comes with minus ten degrees, embracing cities into a wonderful snowy white blanket. Is there any horror movie in which a ghost used ice knife and penetrate the jeans? I have this nightmare in every winter. Don't worry I am not the only one, minus 25°C wind penetrates any jeans and other protective clothes. This leads to nightmares!

However, But this winter nightmare is well paid by winter sports, especially SKI. Don't miss this chance to learn and enjoy SKI. The beautiful white Ski areas, clear blue sky, bright sunlight and warm glue wine are a feel of being in heaven.

Then comes the gray season. Unlike India, gray is not that famous here. The infamous season is so frequent that every another day is a rainy day. No, it does not rain *cats and dogs*, the rain is low and lower is the sunlight. Completely different season compared to the one we experience in India. Unlike Germany, in India, we long for the monsoon. Moreover, when it arrives, it brings along excitement, engagement and ecstasy. Monsoon is associated with chai (tea), samosas (fried vegetable triangle Indian snack) and pakora (Indian fritter). Grey is the colorful season in India that one enjoys sitting in the balcony with a cup of tea and one of the Indian snacks. Grey weather is not liked in Germany. People use a light color or transparent curtains because of this weather.

I was a toddler and yet to explore German weather. Day temperature drops sometimes so quickly and seems as if it is being controlled by the Stock market. Carry a dick jacket whole day and do not feel to use it and if you by chance miss to carry it, trust me it is the worst day it feels like in a war without arms and without protection. After that one single mistake, one can be ill for a whole week.

The best season is the summer, the days are still hay until 10 p.m. as it is on the north side of the equator. Germans wait for summers, unlike Indian. Long days, after 5 pm in office one has an additional half day to enjoy the day till 10pm. On the contrary, in winters, the day ends by five o clock in the evening. Coming from India, I know that days in summer are ought to be longer and in winters days are shorter.

Before leaving for work, it is always recommended to check for the weather forecast. The climates here are very vulnerable, making body more prone to catch the illness. If it is sunny, it is not necessarily warm. Moreover, southern and eastern part of Germany is famous for pollen allergy, one is liable to get an allergic infection. The infection is seen very common among Indians. Better, be prepared with suitable medicines.

Doctors are exceptions in German punctuality. If one has an appointment with a physician at 10:00, there are microscopic chances that he will meet at 10:00. At clinics, they give appointment to many people at the same time.

*Don't ask me why ?*

Most of the time one hour is just a waiting time, even with an appointment. Private insurance clients get VIP treatment and some clinics only take private clients.

B-Side of German culture is punctuality with a tolerance of maximum 5 minutes. German come on exact time even in private meetings. Many a times I have experienced that my guests came 10 mins early and waited outside my apartment or in the car and rang the bell on the exact time. A reminder is not required for a meeting after 3 weeks, It's good to remind, but they take all meetings seriously.

It was a shocking experience when I saw alcohol available everywhere from main railway station to cinema to grocery store. I love Beers and for beer lovers its heaven. There is no restriction on alcohol in German culture. I think in future, alcohol can also be provided directly from pipes to homes, just kidding but why not. Though alcohol consumption level is too high, still misbehaving by drunkards is very rare. At dinner, they like to have wine. 6PM is the dinnertime and after that beer or drinking time. On everyday basis, evening dinners are cold and non-cooked food.

In south of Germany, there is a tradition of KEHRWOCHE. It is a kind of cleaning responsibility in multi-apartment houses which means for one week Kehrwoche family is responsible for cleaning of common places like garage, street stairs etc. While snowing it's a big and annoying task and one needs luck. Being unlucky, I had Kehrwoche whenever there was snow and i had to work for long on weekends to clean.

Taxes are too high in Germany but worth to pay. On almost every area, there are kids playing area and well maintained by the government. Initial days were full of eye-opening days as everything was automatic and totally new for me. Parking garage gate opened with remote control, automatic light systems. Doors open and closed automatically. Public parking buildings are fully automatic and there is a single person who vigilance 500 cars via cameras. No Bus conductors, Bus driver take care of everything. He has fully automatic driving and ticketing system. With no hassle, drivers handle driving as well as conducting. To promote this automation, multiple automatic ticket machines are implemented and standard ticket counter charge extra so that customer shifts to an automated system. At city petrol station, a single person can handle complete station which has fuel filling, shop, car cleaning and air filling. As all the systems are automatic or customer has to do my own. Even the Police use fully automatic radar system for over speeding. The system called, "Blitzer" takes a picture as well as calculates the fine of over speeding. The penalty is sent via post directly to the person.

Blue color persons aka labors are very expensive. From hairdresser to electric to the plumber, all are busy and costly. A medium level hairdresser charges 25-50€ (approx. 1750 – 3500 INR) for boys haircut and requires a prior appointment. Yes, appointment! Electrician and plumber services start from 50€ (3500 INR) per hour. Yes per hour! It's because they are well trained and did studies of that area.

There is another incident about time. It was summer as I was attending my German training workshop. As the rule applies, teacher, after finishing the lecture advised us to shift our watches to an hour past. Not having a clue, I said, "Mam, we SHIFT watches only when we want to EXCHANGE them. What are you talking about? Why you want us EXCHANGE our watches? Is it some kind of ritual? " Teacher responded, "dear, it is because winters are approaching." You have to shift one hour backward.

*"Why?" In addition, I laughed aloud.*

The whole class kept mom and gave me the weirdest look. I couldn't help but laugh. The thought itself demanded a loud laughter. And, when I saw no one joined me in with the laughter, it got changed into awkwardness. I stopped laughing. And at the very next moment, all of them started giggling, including the teacher.

'Day Light Saving' concept, which I was not aware of. Following the concept, the natives tune their clock an hour past and ahead in summer and winter respectively. But, as Germany and I was fascinating first-fight-and-then-love story. I was embarrassed. It was then I was enlightened with the concept that is practiced not only by Germany, but also by other foreign countries.

Apart from the weather, food is really awesome. Initially Indian don't like German cuisine but after developing this taste it's attract like a magnet. Sugar and salt intensity are lighter than the Indian one. Bakery and Cakes will for sure add extra weight as it cannot be avoided. There is no way to miss German Beer, there is no alternative to German beer. For adventurous food, try Blutwürst which is not a normal sausage, major ingredients are real blood and meat.

Vegetarian people can find food. Fish eggs and other sea foods are considered as a vegetarian meal. So, please ask explicitly them without meat and without fish. Most of the restaurants and office canteen have a minimum vegetarian meal. But in private parties, it's difficult to get. So when invited please acknowledge them. Vegetarianism is increasing day by day and Vegan Restaurant is a new trend. It's not so difficult as in China or Japan to find vegetarian food. Fast food restaurants also have some meat fewer Burgers but don't confuse with cheeseburger as Vegetarian Burger. German has vast range of delicious food and tasting this culture will definitely add extra pounds. But who cares!

*"Food is not rational. Food is culture, habit, craving and identity"* by Jonathan Safran Foer.

# 12. POLICE

## Do Not Catch If You Do Not Want To Get Caught

I find everything associated with Germany to be beautiful, including Police. Style in their walk, grace in duty and sophistication in the talk, to me, any German Policeman is not less than a Hollywood actor. I think "Dabangg" Movie Police officer role and the idea was taken from German police. White as snow and gentle as a breeze, "Polizei" stays like this until they say freeze! At their best, they are your mother and in worse they are the "Polizei". In India, their strong voice and a big belly identify Policemen. They are perceived more as Bollywood villains.

Beauty with a brain is not the only application for girls; it applies to others too including Police. Let me explain.

During my internship in a very small town in Baden-Württemberg south of Germany, I was staying in company guesthouse with two of my German friends. It was a small suburb with only ten thousand residential counts. When I arrived, the natives were overwhelmed to see me the only brown guy among the whites- taking the tour of the town. Their eyes were shouting the sense of attraction item. I almost felt like a beast or Zombie as they were constantly glaring with the sign of suspicion.

I, anyway, marched to our so-called "guest house" which consisted of a small kitchen and a huge drawing hall and no internet service as the cherry on the top! No internet source means zero connection to happy life i.e. no checking of e-mails, no surfing and definitely no more movies. We tried to take a new internet connection but didn't get because we had no address proof of our stay. We were in company's guesthouse and company has to apply for the internet. For poor students like us, the company denied taking. Moreover, the city was too old to house any cyber café. My two friends and I were disheartened. We were left with no choices but the consequences. It was like eating käsespätzle (cheese noodles) without käse (cheese).

*Believe me! Living without the internet is much more difficult than Diet.*

One of my German friends, with the motive of knowing more about the town, decided to take a tour to get more acquaintance and digest the fact of no Internet connection. While I decided to stay back at the guest house after the training, he every evening roam around the city to find something I have no clue of. On one sooner day he rushed to me with most cheerful voice and said, "Dude, I found a Wi-Fi connection!!!!"

I promptly replied "NO WAY", one could find water in the desert but no cyber café in this city.

He said "Believe me, I know much better, how it works in such cities"

His emotions were similar to that of a small boy, who was struggling to pass the lanes to get his favorite ice-cream and once he got, his happiness is out of the world.

He explained to us that there was much house (didn't understand) of old people and their internet connection or WiFi is without any lock or password. One can simply login and use.

Though I was happy that finally we have discovered the internet connection, I still glued with my decision to stay in the guesthouse and not to use the unknown Wi-Fi, in spite of my friends stressing on to come along. I thought using someone else's connection could be considered as information breaching and would promote me to the unwanted consequence. I am always watchful of such things, being international, It's better to be careful with such things, as there are thousands of unknown laws, which one can break. On the contrary, my friend is a kind of whimsical. His each day passed through training and then he used to hop over the pre-owned Wi-Fi connection.

He managed to find the connection every day, never got caught, and there was no stopping to his internet lifestyle. He used to check emails, downloads movies, watch movies and what all not on his device. I desperately wanted to know that Wi-Fi and enjoy the bliss of 10mbps Wi-Fi connection, but my judgmental skills held me to a stagnant pole.

It is human nature when you see someone happy with something you longed for, it automatically propels you to achieve that 'something' with the same employed means. Finally, after struggling with our thoughts, my another

German friend and I decided to go along with the friend for Wi-Fi hunt.

It is dark after 5PM as it was a winter evening and after drinking two cans of beer, we took our laptops fully charged and drove to find the Wi-Fi. It felt like we were going to forest to hunt a wild animal, which I never did but the animal channels gave me this feeling. While we were in the car, I found a Wi-Fi, which was an unlocked connection, which according to my expert friend was not giving that appropriate speed. He asked me to have patience and assured me with higher mbps speed and the best connection. After all, who knows better, he was our WiFi hunting GURU?

At last, he parked the car before a house where speed was appropriate, and quickly without doing much ado, we opened our laptop and consciously connected the unlocked Wi-Fi of that house. There was complete silence in the car except for the noise of pressing the keys on the keyboard. We were so indulged in the act that we hardly cared what was happening around us.

Like other Germans, my friend considers each tiny detail before going for Wi-Fi hunting, he told us to take headphones so that no one can disturb other in the car. Amazing, Germans are excellent in organizing and planning, sometimes they spend more time in planning than in doing that activity.

After few hours, we heard a siren of Polizei approaching towards us. Having no clue, we guessed the Polizei may be on regular rounds. I asked my expert friend that if he came across such patrol in the past few days. Being busy with the internet and its offerings, he neither bothered to answer nor I further bothered to ask. Moreover, that planning of having headphone reduces the sound on Polizei Siren.

Suddenly two officers knocked on the window and shouted FREEZE! I was stunned, anxious and frightened all at the same time. At first, I couldn't understand what was happening as my eyes were beamed into the laptop screen and couldn't adjust to the outside darkness in the fraction of seconds. Therefore, it became difficult to understand who was knocking at us, but when the voice came again "FREEZE!"- It was freaking situation.

*Then, I understood the meaning of freeze. When Police is in serious mood, it does not matter how handsome the Policemen is. I was cold but only from my face expression, inside sweating already started because of fear.*

We lowered the window to ask what law we had breached as we were oblivious to the passage of time. One of the officers raised his voice louder and pointing the stick or electric gun and dragged us out of the car. Throughout my life, I had never seen a gun for real, and that moment too arrived! Truly I still don't remember, was it a gun, electric gun or police stick. I was totally faded. The other officer took our laptops, seized them and tied our hands. We were deeply upset and agitated.

While the two officers were discussing, they ordered us to kneel down with our hands tied. We were then taken to the police station in that siren sedan. I was totally blank, the only thing I remember was that they took me in Mercedes-Benz rest all was dark for me. It's like when you are knocked down in boxing and remember the flying stars for me, I just remember the "Benz Star". You know, we were knocked down not by Police but because of our fear.

They parted us into three different rooms as we were still in shock. I felt lost! After some time, they asked if we need water, tea or coffee. It was another shock and surprise for me. Was he kidding me, asking me for Tea? It was unlike the Indian police station to house beverages for a lawbreaker. No, I have never ever been to an Indian police station, but have heard blood-curdling stories about it.

They interrogated us individually in a different room. He asked me the routine questions- who you are, where you from, etc. in the German language.

OMG, I was so much in fear that I totally forgot that I knew how to speak German. I was not able to speak a single word in German, leave German apart I forgot my English skills that very moment.

I asked my God, HEY GOD HELP ME IN GERMAN, So that I can convince them.

*God replied, "SON! Even I don't know German Language"*

Polizei was asking me again and again and I was replying like a stammer. They saw my fear and gave me water to drink. After having that sparkling water they gave me, I got some energy and started giving answers. I told them I am Mechanical Engineer, and I am here doing studies and here for my internship. All of the questions and the fact of me being engineer were approved by the officer, except the one.

He checked my passport which says I am in Germany for the Masters of "Computational Engineering" studies. (Computational Engineering is a field of digital simulation and part of mechanical studies). The officer misunderstands that I am an IT or Computer science student. Being Indian and studying computational engineering, he thought that I am an INTERNATIONAL HACKER or HACKER GURU and other two Germany friends are my assistants.

According to him, we were a team of hackers, programming some codes in the dark to hack someone's bank details and have an online robbery.

*Waaw, was it not a side effect of Hollywood movies? I am sure that officer was a fan of such movies that's why he interrogated us in such way.*

Why he was thinking like that? Three suspicious boys, in the dark, new to the town, with 3 laptops, moving the car to and fro to find the best connection, the scene was perfect and self-explanatory to declare us hacker.

I confronted many times that it is our mistake to use someone else's WiFi connection and explained the difference between computational and computer studies. He continued to drill me down with all the stupid questions just with the motive to catch the fire out. I said we had no internet connection at our guest house and so, we were using the free Wi-Fi to just to download free movies. I was repeating the same sentence 100 times just to ensure and convince him but I failed.

I was the brown guy and I was the biggest target. German Polizei is very particular about such things. I was the head that led the hacking team, according to what officer was imposing continuously.

The situation was getting fierce and I almost fell for pitfall situation. I explained all Indians are not IT engineers and not HACKERS! It was then I gathered my Indian courage to ask him to check my credentials through my course professional, and inquire my university website to have a clear idea of what is Computational Studies.

With hours of arguments with the officer, finally I got him convinced that I was not a HACKER!

I felt like winning a teddy bear in the fun fair machine after spending 100s of coins. Same way I won by answering 100 repetitive question by Polizei.

He cross checked the interrogation statement of each one of us and gave us the clear chit. But, they are Polizei after all! No suspicion gets that easy passage from their hands. They took our laptops, get it checked by their IT department, and inspected the guest house if they find any other IT gadget. After the inquiry and investigations were over, my heart got a tune to the normal pumping and now, I can breathe again.

Then at last, officer ended the conversation with a note that gave me the clear message. He said, "When a person keeps the door open it does not mean that he wishes to welcome every passerby in the house. You have to first knock the door and ask whether you are welcomed. As a responsible citizen, you must have asked before using the Wi-Fi connection and have avoided the situation. And, if you don't then you are liable to be caught as a thief".

Those words just hit my guts till date! He was absolutely true.

We were lucky that they did not charge a case against us. We were the saviors of the day. After both the officer had left, there was a complete silence in the guest room. After the nail-biting situation was over, we opened a bottle of beer and after five minutes the silence broke into laughter. We laughed aloud for many reasons. Our laughter denoted victory, fear, foolishness, and us being a coward.

Do remember, if any device catches Wi-Fi signal accidently, avoid any unnecessary advantage. Else, it may blow up. Trust me no one wants to get into any Polizei interrogation and investigation. I am saying this on behalf of my experience. Although the officers do not hurt physically, the situation gets mentally upset. Those five hours in the station was nearly like a hell for all the three of us. So, do not catch any connection if you do not want to get caught by the Polizei!

*Apart from jokes, I love German Police (have to write to save myself)*

# 13. FRIENDS

"*What is a friend? A single soul dwelling in two bodies.*" *by* Aristotle.

But what happen if one's soul dwells in dozens of friends. I have many new German and Indian friends in Germany and my old n gold Indian friends from India. After so many cultural shocks, my life was still normal. Let me share feelings of my friendship with Germans.

*At first, who the hell says that Germans are not friendly!*

"Casting pearls before swine" proverb fits perfectly to those who don't understand Germans. Throwing pearls at pigs is of no use, because they won't know that they are valuable. And I am not a swine who don't know this valuable pearl.

Germans are straightforward but it doesn't mean that they don't have fun or they don't make friends. Before landing, I had heard from many and read online all these rumors that it's difficult to survive and live in Germany for a foreigner because Deutsche is not open minded people. All fake !

Anyhow, my experience was different. I was little afraid and nervous before meeting them for lunch, shopping or parties. So, in initial days, I was very formal. I was asking 100s of questions to them about their culture, country, working etc. and I was telling them about my country, which I am sure they never understood. Some of them were making jokes on India and Indian, fun is always good but teasing is different.

Our communication was in English and they shifted to German while making jokes. It was hard to analysis who is teasing and who is doing in a funny ways. My relation with them was actually bogus as I was not myself. I used to behave or react in a manner, which they would like or want to hear. It's like impressing a girl in her way and after some time one does what she wants. I wanted to be James Bond and girls like what Mr. Bond does. So, I finally decide to be myself and that was my kickoff day to find true friends.

From that very moment my life changed drastically, I made many good friends and pissed many people who were teasing me because of my nationality. Not all are alike, I just had to just filter the best out of the lot.

Meeting them regularly on personal end helped a lot to understand them. I invited them to Indian dinner and snacks. They invited me to Christmas, New Year and other festivals too. Sometimes, I felt they are like coconuts, outside they looked hard and but inside they were soft & sweet.

My formula was to be myself + spend quality time with friends + filter people whom I didn't like. I used this formula and made long terms friends.

*Friends Forever perfectly fit to German Friends!*

Having Indian friends in Germany was butter cake. Being outside form Indian, I liked whatever is from India. I cooked, studied, worked, celebrated and did all other activities together with my other Indian friends. When I was ill they acted as my mother too. The other side of staying only in Indian group is that you mix less with your international friends. Though you spend your time well but get very less exposure to the foreign culture. Here I would suggest spend time with international friends too and try to integrate. It helped me a lot to understand and live a happy life it will help the readers too.

Indian friends from India will always remain the most exquisite friends of my life. They were my long distance companion. Though, I had to filter many online friends who jest wanted to kill time. I totally loved the feeling when my old friends would talk to me over the phone some day and would sound completely jealous of my life back in Germany. The number of photos I put up with my other foreign friends, the number of check-ins that I did started skyrocketing.

Whenever there was a party at my place or in my hostel, I would get some pictures clicked with my friends, upload them on social media, and tag all my friends in that. The act would result that my friends from home would call me up and sound all burnt, parched and bitter about the fact that I was partying, that too in a foreign location and that too in GERMANY! The place where there are glamorous cars, and the country, which is known for its technology! I would snort, and tell them that such parties were an everyday affair. I liked showing off, and would not lie about it. I think it is not just me, I think that every student or every person who has gone out of his country for higher studies does this sort of a thing at some point in his life. Don't judge me; I am sure all have such friends as well.

Everybody paints a pretty picture of the life in other countries. Everyone starts behaving as if everything is rosy, and there is nothing, which is wrong or has adverse affect of the world out there. Let me tell you the aftermath of such parties and so called happy life which most of the time remains untold. Every party calls for after party chores i.e. cleaning part: cleaning the dishes, clothes etc. Thinking of having maids is out of the question.

But the part which I like the most about it was the freedom that I could enjoy when I was there. Having your freedom and being your own boss is a completely different feeling altogether. In India, most of our parents put curfews, and they usually are until 8 PM.

But, here in Germany, it was not like that. I could roam around the town for as long as I wanted to, and would return home late at night, and there was nobody to taunt me. There was nobody to tell me that I was not arriving home on time, and there was nobody to tell me that I was not "behaving like a good, cultured child". I was a free bird in here, and I was flying away into the sky!

I used to log on to Skype to talk to people back home, because honestly, who can afford those long international calls? Before, when I was in India, and would log on to Skype to see, even though half my friend list would be sitting there, nobody would even send me a single message asking me how I was doing. Nobody would even bother with a single Hi, and when I say this, I am even including all the guy friends that I have. But then, things were changing. All the girls in my hometown who would not even look at me on the street would ping me and shower me with calls all the time. They would give me a call, and would act all sweet, and me, grabbing that one chance, would latch on to the conversation.

The best friends started calling me the "German Shepard" and they would not stop their fun even if I begged them to do so. These were my true friends, and they were the same with me no matter what! Even if I someday become the richest guy on the planet, I am sure that these are the people who would still come to my huge mansion and would compare me to a dog. And I cherished these friends, and shared all of my life there in Germany with them. They were the ones who knew the real picture and they were the ones who knew the real me, and I was not going to let them go.

Whenever I used to go back to India to visit my parents, all these true friends of mine whom I knew right from my school days would come and pick me up from the airport. My parents never used to come, it was always my friends who would come. I remember that once I had come back from Germany, and the same people had come to pick me up and the first question that they asked me was if I had got them any alcohol from Germany. And I had not! They charged me for it. After all the custom duties that I had paid them, I was finally taken in the car, and they immediately announced were that they were all in the mood to drink as I had come back from Germany after a really long time, and this was nothing short of a festival for them, and they wanted to sit and celebrate my arrival.

The airport is a long way away from my house, and while we were going, we thought that we would stop at some

Dhaba on the highway, and have our share of fun. But, we were scared too. There were a lot of police raids that were going around at that time, and we did not want to get caught on my very first day back in the country. So, we went to some discreet place, and bought some beer, and just when we were about to raise the can to out the mouth, we heard this police van that was coming towards us, and out heart popped up in our mouth.

*We were shocked!*

And we just got rooted to the spot there! A constable had come out of the car and was heading towards us, and our minds were racing on what to do next. One of my friends then got up and tried to be friendly with the potbellied police guy, and explained that I had just come from "outside", and they just wanted to celebrate my arrival and that's it! We tried explaining to him that we meant no harm and will not cause any kind of a nuisance, but will just drink. Do you think it worked? Nope. The constable gave us this one dirty looks and told us that the friend who had come from "outside" will be thrown "inside" the jail if he does not get away. This was our clue. We ran from there and never returned to that place every again!

Germany did give me a lot of opportunities to grow and prove myself. When I was in college, and trying to complete my graduation, I was a "nobody", and people did not even know me. Life shifted from "nobody" to "somebody".

Well said by John Burroughs

"A somebody was once a nobody who wanted to and did."

# 14. GERMAN LANGUAGE

*Der die das... der die das...der die das!*

A<small>DDDDEE!</small>

What one can imagine with this hard tone word. While working late in the evening in the winter time when after 5PM everything is dark and most of the colleagues left for the day. I was working with full concentration in office as I stuck with some concept implementation.

While taking off, one of colleague loudly said "AADDDDEE!"

I ducked spontaneously for safety purpose. I felt like he warned me BE CAREFUL! He came to me and asked me in a curious way,

*What happen?*

*I strongly reply, you tell me what happen? What you said?*

*He laughed a lot and replied I just said AAADDDDEE which means "bye".*

*WTF_§X$%X& §$X%&X !!!*

In which language a sweet and light word like "bye" is pronounced in so hard tone. True it is in South of Germany.

Let's go back to understand the important of the local language and its dialects. One cannot communicate with people in there without knowing the local language, and learning Germany in the few days that I was left with before going over there was impossible. I had no clue how to manage without knowing how to talk to the people over there. I was sure that I would be lost and will be ridiculed by everyone around. Of course, there would be other international students around in the university, but the majority of the people would be from Germany itself, and to communicate with them, I had to learn German.

In countries like the United States of America, people speak English, and even though the accent might differ, it is not like people will not understand a language at all! That is one advantage while going to countries like the United States and all, because at least the language is something that does not have to worry about.

So, before I went there, I tried watching all the German films that I could. Nope. It did not help. That was like biting way more than what I could chew. Diving directly into films was a wrong decision, and I failed!

I started again by resorted to the normal online tutorials and small books that I found in the bookshops near home. The biggest problem when I was learning German was the pronunciation. The words are so tough, and I could not twist my tongue accordingly. I tried so hard, but there was nobody to guide me, there was nobody who would tell me that this is how it is supposed to be pronounced, and there was nobody to tell me that I was wrong. It was like my history class all over again! I had the same issue with History, and I still suck at it. History repeated now in German language and I failed again!

I did not want fluency in German, I just wanted to learn enough to communicate with the shopkeepers there, and tell them what I needed. Now this time I searched German teacher and was getting personal classes. OMG! With so many grammar rules like Akkusativ, Dativ etc. I was jammed in "der" "die" "das" and my old German teacher was teaching me only grammar. And again I failed!

My failure in German language was like Pakistani cricketers failed against Indians in the world cup. They failed not because of talent but because of fear of failure!

So, with this apprehension and cloud over my head, I decide not to be afraid of this language and went to Germany without learning it. I thought that once I reach there, I would slowly learn it by talking to the students who will be there. Some of my roommates who were there knew German, but their English was just manageable. Therefore, for the first few weeks, I just tried to talk to them with Basic English. But, my expressions and sign language helped us the most. That time I understood how effective this sign language is, if a 2-year kid can understand my signs then why not Germans. I decided to master the sign language. Just Kidding!

I slowly started learning German from them. I started learning with the yes and no of the things, and those friends of mine were explaining things to me as if I was some small puppy, and they, my master.

Languages are entertaining if you have the interest to learn and enjoy them. German is a very funny language. It usually happens that some of the words in other languages mean something else in other languages, and me, being the kid that I used to end up laughing at all those words that had a different name.

Actually, if you learn German with heart, it is not that tough. A right motivation and the right kind of approach towards it will win the race of language. And It is for all Indians. This is because the grammar and the formation of the sentences that are mostly used in German are more or less the same as that of "Sanskrit", so it is easy for most of us to learn and understand it. And not only the Grammar that is involved, most of the German words have been derived from Sanskrit. Since Sanskrit is very similar to Hindi and many of the other languages that are spoken in India. It will be very easy for us Indians to learn and speak German without any hassle at all.

I was learning and using it, and knowing the language partially itself is a fun. Once I planned to meet my Indian friend "Ashish Sethi" on city center of Stuttgart. We both were on same level of German Language. I called him the time we planned to meet.

*I asked him "Where are you? I am in city Centre (which is a huge shopping Centre)"*

*He replied, I am also at city Centre.*

*I asked him which street (Street = Strasse in German Language)*

*He saw nearby and read the name of street on Pole and replied*

*"Einbahn-strasse"*

*"Ok, which number?" I asked quickly.*

*"Don't know, it's just written Einbahnstrasse" he said.*

*Dr.G*

I looked around me and found that I am also on "Einbahnstrasse". I was happy to know that we are on same street. As we had flat rate telephone so we were taking continuously.

*I told him, "Great we are on same street, please tell me in which street number you are?"*

We didn't find the number and searched on google maps but we were not able to find the street in google map too.

Later on, I asked a person and he laughed a lot on us and said *Einbahnstrasse* is not the name of street, it means "One Way Street" for vehicles. We comprehended that we were on two different streets and our language little knowledge ended up on this situation.

About funny part words that I got to hear in Germany. One of the most common words that we use in our everyday life is "Bye". Now, we say that to everyone when they are going away, right? Bye, all over Germany it is pronounced as "chooooze" or "Choozlee". And this is something foul in Hindi. (It means SUCK), and when we were kids back in college, we would use it very often to abuse or insult the people around us. When I first heard this word, I doubled up with laughter, and could not stop laughing! I just found it too funny, but eventually I started using it more and more often.

When I used to be on the phone with my parents, and they would say a bye to me after all the drama over the phone too, they would say a bye, and I would reply saying "chooooze". This, in the beginning was so awkward for me, as my parents did not understand that, and in turn would find it offensive. I was helpless! I could do nothing about this because I was just used to the language over there, which is why I used to use that particular word.

Even with my friends, I started using the word "chooooze" more and more often, and all of them reacted in the same damn way. They had thought that I was abusing them, and in turn, without doing anything at all, I used to get an earful of insults from each of them just because I used a single German word with them! I later on explained to them that it is just how it is, and that I was not abusing or insulting them in any way.

The language fun is not only in communication but also in the shopping, I bought some body cream named "Dusche Cream". After using it for few days, my skin turned red and then I searched about this cream on internet and came to know that it's not a body cream. It's a shower gel!

Magazines were only for watching photos as I didn't want to put extra pressure to read German while relaxing. This became a habit and didn't want to buy magazines in Germany as its a one-minute entertainment to see all pictures. I realized this bad habit when I was traveling to India. I took one free magazine in Aircraft and saw all pictures in just one minute and later on realized that this magazine is in English, I can read and enjoy.

"Lakhawindar" was another Indian who had come there to Germany to study and was also another scapegoat like me. And, his name, being long, was ruined beyond any repair. That poor boy there was helpless! People there would call him "Lack-der-winter" means laughing winter That is so different from the actual pronunciation of the guy's name, that after a while, he stopped trying to explain to each and every person over there that it is pronounced "Lakh. Win. Dhar" All this was of no use.

"Moi Moi" sounds Chinese but its hello in north Germany. "S" is pronounced as "Z" and vice-versa. Ä,Ü,Ö alphabets will help your tongue to do gymnastic. Out of world is "R" and it is pronounced like Rrrrrrrrrrrrrrrr! Don't even try from books. The best way to hear and repeat what they speak.

There was a really funny incident that took place with me that involved this incident that made me laugh and wonder about the variations is languages and what it can actually do to foreigners! There is this word in German "Vorfahrt" that is pronounced as "Foorfahrt". This term is usually used while driving and Vorfahrt means the right of way. If I say other had vorfaht it means he has priority to cross and I have to wait.

In India, it is nothing like that. The person who has the biggest car, or the person who honks the loudest or who is faster than the people who are before him in the lane goes away first not caring at all about anything called rules or regulations.

Back to the story. This happened to me when I was in India for a vacation and was traveling in a car with my friend. My friend was the one who was driving, and I was in the passenger seat on the left side as in India it is right-hand drive. We were traveling in the conventional traffic with cars standing bumper to bumper and people honking their horns, and showing off the speed of their shiny new cars. And as soon as we had a little space to go, there came a guy speeding from the right-hand side of the car and he wanted to overtake the car that we were traveling in. And my friend, being used to the typical Indian style of driving, tried to accelerate and tried to get past the guy, without allowing him to get ahead of us. And as soon he did that, I said "Hey! He had Foorfahrt".

My friend quickly replied don't worry we will do "Phood Phaad", which means beating and breaking in Hindi, and assured me that he will do just that with the guy who dared to overtake us. Now, this was enough to freak me out. I told him that we are not going to do anything of that sort, and will just go on our way. I explained to him that actual meaning of vorfaht, and which is when the realization dawned on him. But, he did not just lap in this bit of information happily. Instead, being the friend that he is, he started making fun of me that I had become a complete sissy after going to Germany and was not my usual old self again.

Even though I knew that no one would actually understand any of the things that I accidentally keep saying in German all the time, I just cannot help it at times! Words just tumble out of the mouth, and I just have to explain everything to them later on.

There is a different kind of fun when it comes to learning a new language. It is fun filled and exciting at the same time, and Germany is a very old language too. There are many dialects of Germany and people from different parts of Germany speak in different accents. One of the dialects is "Schwabisch" which I love to learn and use. It's not because I worked there but because the tone is similar to Haryanvi language where I grew up in India.

German language and on top using local dialects helped a lot to integrate. Delving deep and deep into the language is a fun thing to do, and that was one of the things that made my life more exciting, in Germany.

# 15. BEING INDIAN

*"If opportunity doesn't knock, build a door" by Mr. Milton Berle.*

This quote inspires me always, opportunities may come but why should I wait if I can create one. I learned this from my mentor, teacher and friend "Mr. Tarun Sharma".

Until now I have told about the fun in Germany. I had my share of fun over there, but honestly, the thirst to prove myself was overpowering me. The main reason that I had gone to Germany was to build my career. To prove myself to everyone, my parents, the people who ridiculed me all my life. To those people from my class back when I was in college who had thought that I was good for nothing. I wanted to be successful, and I wanted to reach my goal soon, which is why I actually came to Germany to create my own opportunity.

One of the first things that I gained, after getting out of my parents' house and starting living on my own is – my own identity. Before I came to Germany, I was just known as my father's son and known because of and by family name. I used to carry around this tag everywhere. When I was back home, I was known to people around the town as somebody's son. Or, even when one goes to another state to study or to visit, their city and the place that they come from becomes their identity. I was known as the guy who is from Delhi or Bangalore. But, I wanted that people should know me by qualities. Forget that people in Germany know me because of my family, many of the people cannot even pronounce my name properly! They ruin my name, and murder it in cold blood. It just squeezes the life out of me, and ears will actually start to bleed. It's not that harsh but not easy to digest. After a while, I realized I did same to them, I was not able to pronounce their names properly.

When I told people that I am from India, all that they would ask me was about the poverty in India. The dirty lanes they have heard about and the lack of sanitation and I could see them judging me and my birthplace, when clearly, there is nothing that is remotely close to the picture that they have in mind for India. Thanks to Oskar winning movie "Slum dog millionaire" who helped to build this image.

They were surprised and many eyebrows rose so high that I thought they might disappear altogether when I told them that I had a laptop from the time I was in college. They asked me ridiculous questions like "Oh, you had a laptop? Then you must be pretty rich!" I tried to explain most of the kids in Delhi or Bangalore have a laptop. But, honestly, I should not be the one saying this. I should not be this infuriated just because some people from the other countries do not the complete picture, and still think that India is just a land of dump yards and dusty roads. It is simple. Many of us also think about tribes and children suffering from diseases when anyone says Africa in front of us. Have we been there before? No. But, that is just the picture that we have formed in our heads about the country, and we believe that it is really like that! We do not know that South Africa is actually a country that has amazing skyscrapers and striking industries all over.

In India, even though a person is 22 years old, they do not have the right to take a decision for themselves in many cases. Our schools and colleges, and the courses that we have to do major in, and even the person with whom we have to spend our life with, all are pre-decided and most of the time, we do not have a say in any of them! Looking at the culture in Germany and other developing countries, the kids are responsible for their own actions and are allowed to make and take decisions right from a very early age. This will help them develop a sense of independence and they can even learn from their mistakes! I think it is high time we start doing this with kids in our country too!

I was surprised by the rate I was growing. I was an adult and was behaving like one. With every decision that I took, I used to put in a lot of thought into it, and started being very careful. I was managing everything on my own, and was standing on my own feet, and was not dependent on my parents anymore.

I started coming off the cocoon that my parents had built around me. Before this, all of my actions were based on my parents. They would tell me what to do, and I used to blindly follow it. I always had this assurance that they are there to help with things around. And I guess this is true for most of us. When I was a student also, I had this assurance that my parents will always take care of my finances and whenever I used to run out of money, I would just go and simply ask them for some.

I learnt lessons from my own mistake and took lot of time to establish. It is not mandatory to learn from own mistakes, one can learn from other mistakes too. I was not lucky to learn from other mistakes. That's why I wrote this book with all my mistakes. Other side of coin is that my identity was always linked with my nationality, for me my nation image is much more valuable than my own image. I represent my country, so I took all major decisions keeping my county as well as my own image in mind. When people respect me, then they start respecting my Indian culture and my country as well.

I have seen Indian patriotism during "Indian Against Corruption Movement" by Anna Hazare. I was always interested in politics from the time I was a kid. Rather it was a strange thing, actually. When all my peers in schools used to run from their tuitions every evening to watch Pokemon, I would switch on the TV and watch the News. Actually, it started with my father not letting me switch on the TV. I am honest now. My dad would act like the human remote control that would not listen to anyone else, and I used to sit and watch News channels all the time. And as I grew up, it became a habit, and increased my interest in politics. I would actively take up sides and would stand up for causes. Apart from having a girlfriend, this probably was the only thing that I ever took seriously.

When a person leaves for another country, people usually look at him as if he or she is a traitor. Many misconceptions that people become Westernized or that they stop thinking about their country and social needs follow them everywhere they go, and I hate to admit it, but this sometimes is true. I mean, we all have that one cousin or that one friend who has gone abroad, and has come back to India screaming insults at the country and criticizing everything right from a blot of ink to the judicial system in the country. Not to forget, they do all this with an accent.

Sometimes, it so happens that when we start living in a foreign country, we tend to get involved in the political issues and the problems in that country more than we get involved in the political issues of our country. But, for me it was different. I was still following all of the happenings in India even when I was Germany and would look up the News from time to time. All this interest actually originated from me binge-watching News from childhood.

There was a corresponding event of India Against Corruption that was taking place in Germany as well, and I found out the details about this campaign. As all Indian festival are celebrated on the weekend in Germany so this campaign was also planned on Saturday. All of the Indians who had heard about this movement and wanted to support it were showing their support while in Germany by spreading awareness, and holding meetings and even on social media. I was an avid supporter of this movement and was doing everything that I could do to make it a success.

There was a parallel movement that was happening in Munich and all the Indians living in Germany who wanted to support this were meeting in the center of Munich, which is the center of Germany. While I was at this movement was the first time that I ever felt so patriotic! When I went to the square where this program was supposed to take place, I saw a couple of hundred individuals who had gathered there. Frankly, I was surprised to see this number. And the numbers kept on increasing. After a while, there were four hundred of them, and then five hundred of them. It was so surreal! I always knew that I was an Indian (I still am, actually), but I never felt it as strongly as then.

I went there, along with a few of my friends and other supporters, and traveled to Munich from my city in trains, carrying huge banners and posters supporting Anna Hazare's movement. We also wore those really cool caps that Anna Hazare support and were very enthusiastic at that time. We prepared speeches, and talks and made slogans. The meeting was going to happen at the very center of Munich. Like how Connaught Place is the center of Delhi or how Koramangala is the center of Bangalore, All Indians, gathered together in the middle of Germany, united by one cause. As nowadays, our PM Modi addressing Indian in foreign countries and we see the enthusiasm of Indian. The similar picture we have seen in this movement in Munich and most important it was not organized by anyone, it was feeling of being Indian and does not matter which city, I was still INDIAN!

We got to the end of the program by singing the National Anthem. While I was singing "Jana Gana Mana... ", I was touched to see that little kids, who were born and brought up in Germany were trying to sing along with us, and I felt so good to see them trying to adapt our culture and our habits even though they have not been exposed to it that much! There were all standing with their heads held high, and it was such a proud moment for me.

In my opinion, everyone, whether from the technical side or the non-technical side, one has to experience life in a foreign country at least once in a lifetime. I come from a middle-class family, and I know it is tough to manage the cost of living in another country, but it's a good deal to build a bright career.

# 16. GERMAN SOCIETY

## A Beautiful Patchwork

*"A nation's culture resides in the hearts and in the soul of its people" by Mahatma Gandhi*

I lived in many cities, town and villages to taste German culture and it can only be done while living with them. There is a huge cultural difference between Germany and India, mostly when it comes to social life. I got this wonderful experience from German families, friends, neighbors etc. The perfection reflects in their personal life too. If I ask any address to German, if he don't know he would reply quickly "No! I don't know" and if he knows he explain with all minute details.

I was invited to a lot of parties and get-togethers by my German families and friends. When I went to these parties, I had noticed how different this culture is from Indian. Things that usually do not matter in India tend to be a huge deal in other countries.

The families in Germany are not as affectionate as Indian families. Don't get me in the wrong way. They all love their families as much as we love ours, but the difference is just that they do not show it in the same way. Our Indian families believe in showing and showering love no matter where they are, or whom they are with. But, in Germany, people give a lot of importance to manners and etiquette.

Girls greet Boys by hugging on each side and chick kiss. Indian Bollywood copied this tradition on stages. Boys greets with hand shake or gentle hug. It's still confusing for me to do twice or thrice the check kiss while greeting some girl. As some facilities do left and then right and some left-right-left.

Another thing that to keep in mind is to let a person with own personal space. It's just opposite to India. Indian friends can come any time and does not matter with other person plan. No formalities, either I had to cancel my plan or I had to add them to my plan. For Indians, asking friends for an appointment is just stupid. If I ask, what are you doing in December first week Sunday, may I come? The reply is "Are in your mind, why are you asking, just come or ask me 1-2 days before." Very rarely we plan long dates. Asking Parents for the meeting is NO GO! As most of Indian live with their parents. This question does not apply to a family member.

The lifestyle people lead over there is much more on the broader side, and we do not get to see that in many families in India. For example, divorce is a very common thing over there, and unlike in India, a divorced couple is usually in good terms. This is not such a common thing in here. In India, we do not see people getting divorced as easily as people from the West. We would rather deal with all problems with the marriage than taking a divorce. Even when it comes to things like love-Childs, or having kids from a previous relationship or marriage, people just take them very casually. We just cannot imagine all that in here. A "Patchwork" family, which means a kid from different partners, live together and it works really well, depends on family too. Such concept is hard to find and accept in India.

The thing over there is people do not complicate things. They do not over think as much as we do, which is a good thing in many ways. I mean, I have seen a seventy-year-old man having a girlfriend and being in a live-in relationship with her, but twenty-something kids in India have not even heard of a live-in relationship. The way people think here is much broader, and I think it gives much more space to a person's individuality in a way.

Bottom line, never asks a German about their personal life, because it can be more complicated and can hurt other person. Families there are more nuclear in nature, and it is better to avoid these topics to have a decent conversation.

Neighbors are most important people in Germany! Sometimes important than own boss in the office. There are 1000s of rules which one can break unknowingly in the apartment. Like on Sundays or public holidays, it is not allowed to use a vacuum cleaner, drill or any machine which makes noise. Being Indian we do most of our stuff on Sundays. But Sunday is a family and silent day for Germans. If one breaks such rules and disturb the neighbors than they can call Police and rest is clear.

Trees are not allowed to cut and neighbors watch out how to behave with own kids. Neighbors can be a Spy for you. Beating kids or not taking care of own kids can create problems. So it's better to have good relation with neighbors so that they can understand our culture and vice-verse. A common dustbin or parking place can also create big problems. Understanding the garbage types and garbage system in Germany, took me same amount time to understand the movie "Inception." Reading for weeks and lot of discussion with friends only helped me to understand both - the movie and garbage system in Germany

*Intercultural Guru Dr. G advice all Indians, that after shifting invite neighbor for a coffee or wine to know each other and develop a nice relation.*

To understand this culture I had to be part of it. I used a method, which is to invite them for Indian dinners, and it worked. After some time, as they invited me too. Once, I was invited to a dinner at my boss place. As I was not aware of the place, he told me we would pick me from office. In hassle, I didn't think of taking any gift or flower. Being a nice boss he gave me signals too. He stopped at the shopping center for himself to buy something and just bought a few bananas, I didn't understand why he just bought some few mini bananas.

*I don't know why I didn't use my brain, one side I think like Sherlock and other way it is like Mr. Beans.*

And happened what should not. There were other guests too with big gifts and flowers. I was the poorest guy at that time. After that incident I discussed with other friends too and they had the same feeling, it's a big mistake. I had to swallow my own pride. To overcome that incident I invited them many times to our place but still I have that nightmare!

*"Anyone who has never made a mistake has never tried anything new." — Albert Einstein*

I keep reading this message to console me but I still have that nightmare. So, don't forget to take a nice present when invited. If it's a party then they open the gift in front of all which is not normal in India. Spend time to make a handmade creative card or select the right gift. Don't just buy anything for a sake of gifts.

A party without music is not at all a party. It also depends on what type of music and loudness. In a typical north Indian party, usually the music is so loud that one usually cannot hear yourself and have to shout above all of the Bollywood songs that are played. Kids running around and playing, women sitting and gossiping in a corner, and all the men sitting and drinking in another corner. And after a while, everyone gets on to the dance floor and the party goes on till the wee hours. This is Indian way.

In the case of parties in Germany, things just take a complete turn. The parties here are a little on the formal side, so that means that people turn up in suits and fancy blazers, and the women wear ravishing dresses to the parties. There is no loud music and people talk in low tones. They start slowly, with the people meeting and greeting each other in slow tones, and the conversations are started with subtle topics the favorite being cars, of course. Everyone has a glass of wine in his or her hands, right from women to older men who are in their sixties. Even when people get drunk over here, they still remember their manners and the way that they should behave when they are in a public place. Once the alcohol kicks in, the tone of the conversation lightens a little bit and they start talking about all of the funny incidents that they have witnessed or they start off with the games. But hey, these are fun too. The difference in craziness and sensibleness, one can see this craziness in Germany during football matches, Volk Fest, New Year and in October fest.

But be careful! They are sensible even in craziness. Don't be personal or touch someone in party. I made that mistake once, because I was used to doing that in India, and also because I was drunk out of my senses. I just lightly slapped a guy on his head (in a funny way), and a huge scene in front of the whole crowd which was enough for me to snap back to my senses and run away from the party as soon as possible. I apologized profusely and never repeated that again!

Jokes, are a part of any Party. All the Indian things that we do in here like pulling each other's leg, or making fun of people when in a party are a big NO-GO in German culture. Birthday bombs, or loud singings are not at all common over there. People do have fun in Germany, but in a very German way. As in, they are very formal when they are having fun also. To understand how they have fun, one has to live with them. It's like I cannot tell you the taste for "Shaahi Paneer" in words. Another side of the coin is a no surprise that they find Indian culture too loud and boisterous.

# 17. A ROLLER COASTER TRIP

*City of lovers*

How could we be living in Europe and NOT visiting Venice in Italy? Being from a place where we had an acute water problem, the city of canals was something like a paradise to me. During summers, when the scorching heat would not let us anywhere out of our houses, I remember that I would just sit in my house and watch all of these Bollywood films that were shot in Venice, and would feel happy and imagine myself being in the middle of that splendid city. That is how bad the water problem in my city was, so Venice had to happen.

So, it was all decided. I with a group of friends had decided to go visit Venice in holidays, and float on the water for a while. We had decided to drive down to Venice, and had rented a car. We took a minivan sort of a thing- it was a 7-seater van, and set out. But, when we reached the spot we saw that the so-called seven-seater van was not at all spacious! The last two seats that were there in the van were too small! When I saw them, I remembered the van that I used to travel in when I was in kindergarten, because the size of the seats was exactly that small.

However, we manage somehow, and adjusted our entire luggage in that small, hole-like space. See, this is one advantage of being an Indian. Having traveled in public transport like trains and buses, we can adjust anywhere. Didn't we all see people sitting in even luggage racks in trains and buses? Therefore, off we went to Venice!

There were six of us, 3 other guys (Prashant, Dharmesh and Amit) along with me and two girls (Viktoria and Karuna). And out us, there was only ONE German girl with us, and rest all were Indians. She is nice, blond, beautiful and fun loving girl.

So, how do we Indians start our journey when we are going somewhere? By remembering our Gods- Chanting their name at a very high pitch "Jai Bajranjbali!!", and we started our journey. Now, all the Indians who were present there were used to this thing, but the one poor German girl who was traveling with us was as clueless as ever.

Road trips are total fun. All of the people in the van that night on the way to Venice were laughing and talking and eating and drinking all through the night, and our German friend was someone who was not used to all this. I am sure that she just thought that she had come with some sort of lunatics!

We reached Venice the next morning, and as our journey was long and tiresome, we all got into a hotel, showered (Only the girls showered, the guys did not let a drop of water touch their skin), and slept for a while. We woke up after a while, and set out to party! And since we were on a vacation, and were all in a party mood, we started doing the craziest and most weird things there. We were drinking right in the morning with the breakfast, were watching Rajnikant film clips etc. but, we were just in our own world. Our German friend was slowly getting accustomed to our erratic ways, and she was okay after a while. After all this, we headed out to the city. If I had to describe Venice in one word, it would be WOW! The city is beautiful, with canals and waterways every way. Roads are exchanged by water canals. Cars are replaced by boats and traffic regulations for boats were same as for cars. One can barely find motor vehicles over there, as there are boats and just boats! The best part was that people were actually following the boat-traffic regulations! There were numbers of the boats like there are number plates on our vehicles, and they had a boat as taxis and timings for the boat Buses too.

We saw the entire city through boat rides and the water itself was beautiful. Typical Italian pizza was out of the world, we never had in India. Pizza were very thin, light cheese and big pieces of vegetables and we were enjoying with Red wine. Waaw! Now I know why all the Bollywood directors chose this place to shoot romantic films. It was just magical!

After a day in the city, we went to beaches in and around Venice, and they were equally beautiful and neat. The sand on the beaches actually looked golden under the sun, and there were girls all around sunbathing and I was staring at them pretty shamelessly. Those girls were more beautiful than the city. I tried to show off in front of the girls by playing some beach volleyball too, but nobody took a second look at me.

Our journey was at its end but no one knows what was about to happen. We started heading back to our cold and canal-less Germany the next day, and we had to cross borders for that. To reach Germany, we had to cross Austria only then we could reach Germany, but that was like a free border. So, it had to be Italy, then Austria, and then Germany. It is like going to Karnataka, and Maharashtra and then to Gujarat. So, we had started.

When we got into the car, all our energy drained off which we had when we started the journey. We were all in a very sleepy mood, and nobody was really talking much. We were all people who had never worn sports shoes and had never taken part in any kind of a sport, and suddenly we indulged in so many activities and so many water sports in Venice that out limbs were actually falling off. And we were also sad that the vacation that we had planned so much for, and the vacation for which we had waited for so long, had finally come to an end.

It was the similar feeling, as at the end of the birthday, one waits for the whole year for that one day, for that special treatment that people gives, and then the very next day, there is no conduct.

When we were going there, suddenly I saw some water seeping into the ground near the car. I got down to check what it was, and realized that it wasn't water from Venice, but it was the oil from the engine of the car. Something was wrong. After a while, the engine gave loud noise of grrrrrrrrrrrrrrr, and the car lost its balance! I applied full brakes and from 120 km/hr it came down to snail pace. Then I tried to control the car to reserve a lane and after a while, the car broke down completely. Luckily the next petrol station was nearby and we decided to drive till there and call the rental or service company.

Something unusual happened again! I had no contact number of rental service! I had their office contact from where I picked the car and being Sunday, it was closed!

We checked all the papers and rental contract but we didn't find any service contact. All were eyeing at me!

I called some of my friends in Germany to search on the internet and send us the number, which took almost an hour. A lifetime Lesson was learned that to check all the papers and numbers before traveling, especially in Europe where they check all the papers very carefully before providing the service.

Finally, we called up the rental company of the van, and they gave us the number of some other service center. When we called up the service center, those representatives told us that they would reach us in another half an hour.

We got out our lazy bodies from the van and suddenly, we were energized! It was as if a lightning bolt had hit us suddenly, and we stood in the middle of the road, with a vehicle that was leaking and was about to break down, and started having fun. Now our mood shifted to an adventurous drive.

While we were singing songs loudly and having fun in the middle of the road, we realized that there were police around us. Some cops suddenly came over and surrounded us, and started interrogating. They asked our passports. It was exactly like a scene from a Shah Rukh Khan's movie. They asked us to show our passports.

Before giving to Police, I didn't check my passport and gave it to him. He opened my passport and saw there was a cash of 500 Euro. I didn't realize but the Police took that in wrong way. I always put some reserve cash and unfortunately, that day I had it in my passport. I had no plan to offer any bribe but it was too late. I explained him many time but was of no use. He interrogated all of us for 3 hours and checked all our bags with all minute details.

They were asking us why we standing in the middle of the road and dancing and singing! After a while they cooled down and were asking us about our trip fun. We told them our story, and then they asked us to resolve our issue and left us. Thank god for that!

Where were these service people now? It was getting cold and late, and we could not sing any more songs on the road, so we called them up. They told us that they are on the way and they have to tow away the van to repair it, and there was no other alternative.

There was no other vehicle for us? What would we do then?

We asked them to give us more options because there was no way that we were going to stay on the road the entire time. We asked them either to provide a hotel for us or to give us another vehicle. They told us that we can take another vehicle from Austria, for readers knowledge we were still in Italy at that time.

We told them we need a car right there! But we were helpless, we were not in the situation to demand. Moreover, it was Sunday and Sunday is like an emergency day in Europe. Nothing is open and no one works even doctors are on leave. Only emergency services are available.

They suggested us to take a taxi to the Austrian airport, which was about 200Km from a break down place in Italy, and that their company would be paying for the fare. I was more than happy! Give an Indian a discount and see the biggest smile on their face. We hired a taxi, and we started to the airport.

Now the driver of the taxi that we had hired turned out to be a sour grape! He had a very bad attitude and a highly grumpy face. While we were yelling, shouting, and playing in that car, he kept on shooting on us with weird and annoyed looks. He was behaving like our schoolteachers.

After a while, the driver told us that he had some work around there nearby, and asked if we can take a detour for a while. We agreed, thinking he probably had some personal business to attend. He drove away from the highway and went into some dark and dusty lane off the highway.

We were waiting in the car, and then after some 15 minutes, we saw some silhouettes around the car. When we got out, we saw that the driver was coming and there were 10 police officers around him.

*Not again!*

My heart almost sank. What was this guy up to? First came into my mind was, whether the guy was caught by Police while smuggling drugs. As this guy behaviors was like a smuggler or Indian Gulshan Grover, and I was pretty sure that he had knocked up some illegal activity and got us into trouble as well.

But the picture was opposite. This guy had thought that we were body smuggler or refugees who were crossing the border of Austria illegally and had went and reported us! Look at the guts!

None of us knew any Italian at all, and the German girl who was there with us knew a little bit of Spanish, and she tried to explain in Spanish to the policemen that we were tourists, and not any kind of refugees illegally crossing the border. Our dear friend, the driver, had apparently told the police people that we were yelling and partying in the car because we were happy to have crossed the border into Austria. In my mind, I had already killed the guy and smacked his head over a hundred times. He handed us to the police to sings and have fun in his taxi! Can't believe! But we were interrogated again!

After the police checked our passports and this time I checked before giving my passport. They were convinced that we were on holiday, they let us go. Although, we had to praise Italy and their food to understand us. Believe me it worked!

They were very understanding, I must say. They clicked pictures with us, and the women among them looked right out of an action Hollywood movie. We got rid of that jerk driver and Police told us not to say anything to this taxi driver as it's his duty to inform us. Being Indian, we continued our singing and told him to do what you wanna do! After a while he understood that we were on vacation and enjoying the mood. Then this guy changed his mode to entertainment and put on his music system and enjoy with us! Finally we reached the Austrian airport, from where we have to take another taxi.

The trip had another surplice for us. This taxi station did not have a 7 seater vehicle, and there was only a 5 seater available. This ride back home was getting worse and worse with each moment. We were not able to adjust in a 7 seater car, how we all can go in a 5 seater. And in Europe, one can't let people sit on lap. We didn't have more energy to face Austrian Police. We somehow convinced one of our other friends to take a train back home, and the remaining five of us drove back to Germany.

There was a terrific rain on the way back home. At one point I was not able to see the road so we had to stop the car again. We came out and stood under one shed. It was not raining, it was like someone was pouring buckets of water on us. We still had last minutes energy and one of us busted and started dancing in the rain. In a second he was completely drench and then we all joined him except the German girl. Who cares! At that time we had great fun!

We changed our clothes and drove back with memories of our most amazing vacation. Next day, we all got cold and fever. We had no guilt of not listening to our lovely and beautiful German friend!

# 18. FESTIVALS

*Being an Indian you will*
*enjoy it more here...*

Many festivals are celebrated in India, and most of them are organized by us - the people. Contrasting to India, in Germany government organizes every festival for the reason to enjoy with people. Festivals are celebrated out in lanes with the motive of engaging people and to enhance the festive mood. Moreover, not all the festivals in Germany are religious. Most of them are party festivals. They are more about letting you free and relieving from stress. Oh man! I love Germany for all good reasons.

## Oktoberfest-The Beer Fest

German Culture = Oktoberfest = the best Beer Fest = Great Fun. A rare combination of beer, leader pants, sexy Dirndls, folks music, big glasses, rides, food, dances, drunken games and on the top all in the fun and safe atmosphere. This is one of my favorite and many international celebrities' funfair events. The worldwide famous beer fest commences at the end of the September and closes in the first week of the October. Munich, South of Germany host this fest and other cities have a similar version of this fest. This festival offers visitors as well as the natives with the world's finest beer. Millions of people come across the world to participate in the festival with full contentment. And, it is not just about the beer, the fancy dresses give a new culture to the Oktoberfest. The different flavors of outfits, folk music and beer on the top make the delicious dish that anyone would fall for it.

Boys dressed up with leather pants with checks shirts and girls wearing the most beautiful frocks "Dirndls", is the Sexy factor of the festival. Being an Indian, when I witnessed it the whole scene gave me an awe feeling. The tents are organized in a scattered manner. It is free to enter, but hard to get the place inside. Each visitor gets a mass (1 liter can) on entering, and the WOOOW view with melodious vibes of folk music. Despite huge rush and beer on the top, the environment is very healthy. There is a rush but chaos and fights are rarely noticed. They know how to enjoy such festival. it is a must visit festival.

# Fasching - A Carnival

This festival officially begins during November in most of the regions in Germany. The Fasching week, which begins before Ash Wednesday, is also known as Fat Tuesday. This is the carnival famous for its festivity and merry making. It is the time to break rules, to dress funny, poke jokes, pranks and make your own time filled with enthusiasm.

More than anyone else, the festival is enjoyed the most among children. On Fasching, kids dress up in their favorite cartoon or fairy tales characters and roam around the city to feel the bliss of freedom.

People do mischief, but it has its own flavor of innocence. I also noticed people imitating Gandhi in Germany, which made me feel proud of my nation in the country as one of a kind. It was a great experience. If you are in Germany for more than a while, do not miss and participate in the festival.

I experienced this festival on my interview for an internship. While, traveling back from my interview, I met a group of people celebrating the fasching week in a bar. Being in the business suit they thought I was imitating any business person and I joined my interview celebration with fasching. There is no barrier to celebrate festivals. It's the best method to mingle with people.

## Homosexual parade

Christopher street day is celebrated as Gay Pride or Pride Parades in Germany. More than five thousand people with big bands celebrate the bliss of being into a special relationship. The gay parade looks very encouraging. No, it does not encourage one to become a gay one-day, but the feeling of respect natives offer to gay is something very unlikely for an Indian visitor. There are so many people celebrating that parade, one can definitely confuse to judge the number of Germany being homosexual. It seems that half of the city is with homosexual but it is not true. There are non-homosexual people who wants to support the freedom.

# Nabada

There is a river called Danube or Danau which is the second longest river in Europe. On second last Monday of July, Nabada festival is celebrated on the river side of Ulm city, where people present their creative handmade boats. They row their boat and enjoy themselves by splashing water over each other, singing melodies and dancing. It is another must visit festival.

# Holi festival

I was amazed to see my Indian festival being celebrated in Germany. The festival of togetherness and equality where all caste barriers are let down is also celebrated in Germany. Taking a leap of faith, German come together peacefully and throwing colors on strangers celebrate this festival same as we Indian do. It felt so homely when I witnessed it for the first time. My love for Germany continued to grow following many such incidents that I still have to know.

# 19. TOURING GERMANY

**BERLIN** - Berlin is one of the 16 states of Germany and it is the capital city. A city of historical importance, it has a population of 3.5 million. Some of the major attractions in the city include the Reichstag, Brandenburg Gate and The Holocaust Memorial. The Reichstag (built 1894); currently housing the German Parliament, which was damaged by a fire in 1933 and was restored after the reunification of Germany. Another historical landmark is the 18th Century Brandenburg gate. It is designed to resemble the gateway to the Acropolis and has a magnificent sculpture of the Quadriga – a winged goddess on a chariot. Among other must visit places are the East Side Gallery, Potsdamer Platz, the Museum Island, Tiergarten and Check Point Charlie.

**HAMBURG** - The St Nikolai Memorial, which was destroyed in the world war, is a place for remembering the victims of the war. The cellar has a vaulted museum that provides information on how Hamburg was destroyed during the Second World War. The Rathaus or City Hall is located in the center of the Old Town. Children and adults alike will enjoy a visit to the miniature railway – Miniatur Wunderland. Hamburg being located at the head of the estuary of the River Elbe has a rich maritime history and the International Maritime Museum is worth a visit. Other places to visit in Hamburg are Kunsthalle Hamburg, The Port, Olsdorf Cemetery and the Great Lakes.

**FRANKFURT –** In the heart of the Old Town is Römerberg, one of Frankfurt's most beautiful squares with the Justice Fountain. A place where one can witness St. Nicholas Church and the Historical Museums. Johann Wolfgang von Goethe, Germany's most famous writer was from Frankfurt and his home Goethe House with the Goethe Museum next door are both open to tourists. The Old Opera House, which was destroyed in the war, reopened in 1981. The 95 meter tall St Bartholomew's Cathedral built of red sandstone in Gothic style is visible even amongst the city's many skyscrapers. The Eschenheimer Tower dating back to the 1400's houses a café and rooms for use by local historical societies. A couple of other places worth visiting include Naturmuseum Senckenburg and Frankfurter Stadtwald.

**MUNICH –** Munich, the capital city of Bavaria is famous for its annual Oktoberfest. One of the most spectacular palaces in Germany – the Munich Residenz consists of three sections the Königsbau, the Alte Residenz and the Festsaalbau. The magnificent and imposing Frauenkirche, the Cathedral Church of Our Lady is built of brick in late Gothic style and has 100-meter tall towers. The central square Marienplatz has the New Town Hall and the Old Town Hall along with the Virgins Column and the Fish Fountain. The Asam Church is decorated with lovely stucco figures. The other notable places to visit in Munich include the 910 acre English Garden, St. Peter's Church, St. Michael's Church, the Cuvilliés Theater, Nymphenburg Palace and Königsplatz.

**KÖLN –** The beautiful city of Köln is situated on the banks of the River Rhine is known for its majestic churches including the Gothic Cathedral of St. Peter and St. Mary.

The Old Town quarters has the Great St. Martin. For all those interested in art the Wallraf-Richartz Museum, the Ludwig Museum and the Museum of Applied Art are highly recommended. Nature lovers can head to the oldest Zoological Gardens in Germany, the Cologne Zoo. Other places popular with tourists include St. Pantaleon Church, St. Gereon's Church, the Cologne Cable Car and the Old Town Hall.

**STUTTGART** – Stuttgart is known for housing the headquarters of Mercedes-Benz, Porsche and Robert Bosch. Car lovers must visit the two museums of these car manufacturers. Schlossplatz flanked on either side by Königsbau and the Kleiner Schlossplatz is the place to visit for shopping. One can get a taste of Baroque style architecture when one visits the Neues Schloss or New Palace. Württemberg Landesmuseum with its collection of medieval art can be seen in the Altes Schloss. Krishna Temple at Daimlerstrasse 61 70372 Stuttgart - Bad Cannstatt (Tel - 07118882014) is the best and must visit place. Other attractions in the city include the Sepulchral Chapel, Schloss Solitude and Killesberg Park.

# CULTURAL TOUR OF GERMANY

Germany has been known as the land of poets and thinkers. It is also the birthplace of Bach and Beethoven, two of the most famous classical composers. Cultural tours to Germany will be a rich experience. Goethe House & Museum in Frankfurt are famous places. Munich is also home to one of the finest art museums one can hope to visit – Alte Pinakothek. There are masterpieces by Durer, Raphael, Rubens and Rembrandt amongst others. The

Germanic National Museum in Nürnberg is the place to visit to learn all about Germany's rich cultural heritage.

# VILLAGE FESTIVALS IN GERMANY

Wine and Beer festivals take place in practically every city and village in Germany. To get a taste of the local culture attends festivals in some of the smaller villages along one of the rivers of Germany. The Almond Blossom Festival that takes place in March in the small town of Gimmeldingen is generally the festival to start the wine season in Germany. The Wurstmarkt takes place in September in Bad Duerkheim. Another lovely time to visit Germany is during Advent. Nearly every village will be hosting a Weihnachtsmarkt. These are street markets held in the town square with open-air stalls. There are traditional dancing and singing that also takes place here.

# RELAXING TRIPS IN GERMANY

After an overdose of culture, take a relaxing trip and commune with nature. Germany has a lot to offer with the Black Forest and the Alps. Visit the spa town of Baden-Baden in the Black Forest with its natural mineral springs. Another great place to relax is in the Bavarian Alps. Head to Garmisch-Partenkirchen, which is at the foot of Mount Zugspitze that offers the most spectacular views of the mountains. Ramsau near the Hintersee Lake is another beautiful Bavarian getaway. Another relaxing place is Cochem. This little town in Mosel Valley is surrounded by vineyards, hills and other small villages.

# ADVENTURE PARKS

Germany boasts of 7 theme parks. Located in Rust, Europa Park is the largest theme park in Germany with 12 roller coasters. Phantasialand in Brühl has a thrilling ride called Colorado Adventure that takes through the Wild West. The star attraction at Heide Park in Soltau is a wooden roller coaster called Colossos. In Movie Park Germany in Bottrop-Kirchhellen gets to explore several different movie sets. Both children and adults will love to visit Legoland which is in Günzburg. Hansa-Park in Sieksdorf has 11 different themed areas including Pirate Land and Adventure land. Holiday Park in Hassloch is partly a park and partly wood land.

# ADVENTURE SPORTS

The beautiful slopes of Bavaria come alive in winter with winter sports enthusiasts. Some of the ski resorts include St. Englmar, Hohenbogen, Bad Hindeland and Zugspitze. These spots are great for skiing, snowboarding and snowshoe walking. Those with more stamina can try cross country skiing in Inzell or Rhön among other places.

Skydiving or jumping out of an aircraft in a free fall and landing with the help of a parachute is a wonderful way of getting a look at the countryside from the air. Novices can experience this through tandem jumps where they are strapped to a professional jumper. Try this at Gransee near Berlin, Eggenfelden in Bavaria and Bitburg.

Bungee jumping involves jumping from a high place while you are secured by a nylon strap by your ankles. The top bungee jumping places in Germany are from cranes. The places for bungee jumping include Stuttgart, Hamburg and Oberhausen.

Hot Air Balloon rides are a great way to see the countryside. You can do this in summer or winter over the Bavarian Alps, South of Munich. You can even balloon over the rooftops in Munich. Another exciting trip involves crossing the Alps into Italy. This is made possible by some unique weather conditions in winter. The beautiful regions of Elbsandstein and Swiss Franconia offer rock climbing.

# 20. TIPS FOR INDIANS IN GERMANY

*T*ips, *rules, advices given in this book are my personal experience. Therefore, there are no references. Its highly recommend to contact Government authorities to know the updated rules and regulations.*

Germany (Deutschland) has 16 states and a popular member of European Union. Biggest city and capital is Berlin. With 82 Million people, the average age is 43.8 years.

| GENERAL | |
|---|---|
| **Emergency Numbers** | 112 – Medical/Fire and 110 Police |
| **Doctors or Hospitals** | Doctors are available on weekdays and with prior appointment. An appointment does not mean that Doctor will see at the exact time of appointment there might be a waiting time too.<br><br>In the case of emergency, one can visit hospital or doctor, if possible prefer to call before the visit. |

| Police | Don't hesitate to contact Government Employees like Police for queries, they are very supportive. |
|---|---|
| Cars | Don't touch or stand along any car. Germans are particular about their car care. Even a tiny scratch on car can make them very angry. |
| Indian License | An international or Indian license is valid up to 6 months of the first stay. After that, it is advisable to transfer to German driving license. While transferring the license, theory and driving exams are compulsory but not the training classes. It is valid only of permanent Indian driving license holder not for learning licenses. Consult with local German Government authorities for any change in law or individual cases. |
| Zebra Crossing | Don't hesitate to cross Zebra-Crossing. Vehicles have to stop and pedestrians have priority to pass. |
| Bicycle | Wear helmet while driving a bicycle. It is a law. |
| Hit and Run | Hit and Run is a crime. Even hitting any stationary vehicle (even in parking) and run is a crime, please call Police and inform about the accident. Its mandatory to stay there till police come. |

| Physical touch | Avoid kicking or touching someone like a friend. Even a small casual bang on head or shoulder could create a problem. |
| --- | --- |
| Que | Have adequate distance from the people in front while waiting in a que. Before the counter there is a line and stop before the turn comes. |
| Internet Download | Online movie download from unknown links is illegal and regularly controlled by Government. Be careful from Paper mafia, they send fake claims for watching online movies and foreigners are easy target from them. |
| Greets | People greet each other on streets even if they don't know each other. It would be nice to know some common German words Like Guten Morgen, Danke, Bitte, Tschüss etc. Always greet woman first. |
| Greeting Way | Hallo. *In general*<br><br>Grüß dich! *Casual and if you know them personally*<br><br>Grüß Gott! *In southern Germany and Austria.*<br><br>Guten Tag. *Hello/Good Day.* |

|  | Guten Morgen/Guten Abend. *Good morning/evening.*<br><br>Moi moi, Guta Morga, Servus. *Various Dialect* |
|---|---|
| **Weather** | Check weather forecasts and it's better to carry Jacket and Umbrella as temperature fluctuate frequently. |
| **First Day** | It's simple to roam and travel around Germany even without knowing the German Language. It's advisable to accompany by German speaking person in initials days. |
| **Punctuality** | In Germany, punctuality is extremely important. It's a common to inform the delay even if it is 5 mins. |
| **Straightforward** | Germans are very straightforward. Don't be surprised to get a direct answer.<br><br>*Once, I sent a nice Christmas gift to a friend and I was surprised to receive an email asking reason for sending the gift.* |
| **Joke** | Avoid too many jokes in initial meetings; it may go in a negative way. Jokes or comments about world wars are most important thing to avoid. |
| **Blowing Nose** | Blowing a nose in public is common in Germany. Don't be surprised if someone does during eating or praying. |

| Toilet paper | There is no water jet in toilets. Only toilet paper are used and toilet papers have to dump in commode. |
| --- | --- |
| **Handkerchief** | Cotton Handkerchief is out of fashion in German. Use Serviette or Soft tissue. |
| **Cold** | Don't shake a hand if suffering from a cold or a cough. |
| **Personal Talk** | Don't ask any personal questions about family, wife, parents, kids etc. till he or she is a good friend. |
| **Shoes** | Use Tracking or Sports shoes only during tracking or doing sports and avoid them in office. |
| **Shopping** | Stores are generally closed on Sundays and holidays. Except Restaurants or some Bakeries. |
| **Food** | Bread is favorite in Germany. There are bakeries on almost every street and every train station, and some of them even open for a few hours on Sundays.<br><br>From milk to yoghurt all dairy products are of top quality with reasonable prices. |
| **Electricity** | Generally there is no cooking gas. Kitschens have electric heating plates. Don't worry, there is no electric cut. Yes no electric cut and no fluctuation of voltage. That why there is no regulator required in Germany. |

| | |
|---|---|
| **Drinks** | Its heaven for beer lovers. Thousands of variety and each one has its own flavor to enjoy. Hot glue wine is a traditional drink and available during Christmas. |
| **Non-Vegetarian** | Eating meat is very common, so please don't ask why they eat meat. For them eating Red meat is normal. |
| **Street Food/ Quick Bite** | • Bratwürst, Döner, Pizza are the most common available food in market.<br><br>• Döner or Yufta (Inform the restaurant for lamb or chicken, otherwise Beef is by default)<br><br>• Vegeterians can have Falafel option in Döner.<br><br>• At many pizza places one can buy a piece (Stück) of pizza, instead of full pizza. |
| **Water** | There are two common types of drinking water.<br><br>• *Mineralwasser or Sprüdel* (sparkling mineral water)<br><br>• *Stilles Wasser (Normal Mineral Water)* |
| **Water Body / River** | Don't throw any kinds of stuff or religious stuff in any water body. It is strictly forbidden. |

| Ketchups | Ketchup at fast food restaurants usually cost. With pizza ketchups are not served. Most of the mayonnaise have egg content. |
|---|---|
| Fish / Egg | Fish and eggs are considered as vegetarian. There is no concept of RED OR GREEN dot (like in India) on products as a symbol of vegetarian or non-vegetarian product. |
| Jelly | Gelatin is used in most of the Jellies. Gelatin is obtained from various animal by-products. |
| Invitation | While invited, take a gift or flowers or a bottle of wine. Don't give carnations flowers (symbolize mourning), lilies or chrysanthemums (used in funerals). Yellow and green flowers are always welcome.<br><br>Germany opens gifts quickly after receiving and in front of the person who brought. |
| Photos | Ask before taking someone's house, car, kids, Photo. |
| Pets | Dogs are well trained. Don't be afraid from them and they are also allowed in public buses, trams and trains. |
| Sim Card | Sim card can be bought at any Internet or telephone shop. There many providers who have international call tariffs e.g. lyca, libera. Internet or Telephone shop are located at Central Railway station or City Center. |

| Bank | Withdrawing money from other Bank ATM can cost extra. Supermarket like REWE also gives cash withdrawal services. |
|---|---|
| **Credit cards** | Credit cards are not common as in US, even many shops do not accept credit cards. |
| **Insurance**<br><br>**(Haftpflicht-**<br><br>**Versicherung)** | It is a must insurance. It is relatively less price, and provides pretty extensive cover. It covers liablility to pay the third person.<br><br>An imperative example is given here to understand the importance of this insurance.<br><br>Just imagine Dr.G is crossing the road and someone called him and he pick the phone. Unfortunately, he don't see the bicyclist coming towards him. The bicyclist crash nearby Mercedes and Bus behind the Merc has to use emergency brakes to avoid the collision. The bicyclist living cost and hospital bills have to be paid by Dr. G. Mercedes repair cost, and also the medical expenses of injured persons in the bus have to be paid by Dr.G. All these things because of that phone call. So don't think it is only for extreme condition. |

| Number | Handwritten number "1" looks like "7" and It is confusing too. In numbers commas and points are used in a reverse manner. Like $ 2.000,50 is two thousand Dollar and 50 cents in Germany. |
|---|---|
| **Numbering System** | Lakhs and crores are not known to Germans. Use Millions or Billions.<br><br>Million = die *Million (In German)*<br><br>Billion = *die Milliarde (In German)*<br><br>Trillion = *der Billion (In German)* |
| **Additional alphabets** | • ä = ae. "ay," as in "Gepäck" (Gah-payk)<br><br>• ö = oe. "u," as in "möchte"(mukh-tuh)<br><br>• ü = ue. "yoo," as in "Büro" (Byoo-roh)<br><br>• ß = ss. "ss," as in "Straßen" (Shtra-ssen) |
| **Leasing a Car** | There are many leasing offers from car makers. One can afford a luxurious car at a monthly rate of approximate 1% of the total car price including insurance. It is like a renting a brand new car for a limited time. |

| Schooling for Child | • For schooling in English medium, international schools are available but requires heavy pockets. Teaching level may vary from school to school, so enquire well before registration. Fee is from 7000€ to 18000€ fee per year.<br><br>• For schooling in German medium, it hardly cost anything. English is considered as a second language. |
|---|---|
| **Play School** | • Various types of play schools are available up to 3 years kids. KITA, Tagesmutter or Kindertagesstätte. Local Jugendamt offices are the best to consult. |
| **Child seat for car** | German law requires child seat for children up to 12 years of age. These laws also apply when riding in a taxi. |

| BUSINESS TRIP | |
|---|---|
| **Dressing** | Dressing is very important during a business trip. Dark color business suit with formal white shirt and Tie are evergreen fashion. No-Go for flashy and shiny material. |

| Gestures | Don't point index finger to someone while talking. Hands in pocket, chewing gums are not in German business culture. |
|---|---|
| Greetings | Exchanging visiting cards is corporate. The firm, brief handshakes at the time of arrival and departure are standard. Addressing a person by family name is important. If the person has Dr. or Prof title than very important to address him with the title like Prof. Dr.-Ing. Thomas Müller. Then call him by Mr. Prof. Müller and in written (Email or document) use complete title Prof. Dr.-Ing Thomas Müller.<br><br>Don't use "SIR" at all. |
| **Business Meetings** | • Germans tend to be analytical thinkers. They take a decision by facts. Feelings and emotions are irrelevant.<br><br>• Business meetings are treated like a serious occasions. Humor and jokes are not so common. It's very important to come with a planned and organized proposal in a meeting. |

| | |
|---|---|
| | • In the first meeting, plan to know one another to gain trust and understand the compatibility.<br><br>• Meetings are strict to agenda's topic and timings.<br><br>• Send company or personal profiles or other relevant data to German colleagues before the meeting. Avoid hard-sell tactics or surprises.<br><br>• Germans value their privacy and personal space immensely. Do not ask any personal questions related to occupation, age, family or children. |
| **Straight forward** | Direct communication is important in Germany – there's no need to bring a comfortable zone or creating situations where people need to read between the lines. Instead, be direct and straight forward. |
| **Compliments** | Giving compliments openly is not part of German business protocol. Appreciating the work is always good. At the end of a good meeting, German signal their positive compliments by knocking knuckles on the table top. |
| **Eye contact** | Eye contact during the introduction meeting is imperative. |

| Negotiation | Following are important points to ensure a positive result during business negotiations:<br><br>• A person's word or verbal confirmation is considered as a promise.<br><br>• A well-researched work with good citations and statistics is usually preferred. A direct approach and clear target are mostly appreciated.<br><br>• Business is hierarchical. Decision-making took place at top level and followed down. |
|---|---|
| | • Decision-making in Germany is a slow and detailed process. Have some patience while getting the first contract. Do not expect significant conclusions or result. Do not force them to speed up this process.<br><br>• Germans are fact and detail oriented. They want to understand every minute detail.<br><br>• Once a decision is made, they don't change it later. |

| | |
|---|---|
| **Conversation** | Personal talks are taboos. One can talk about sports hobbies, weather, Cars, architecture etc. Talking about beer or about the local bear is always an interesting topic for German. Anything related to World Wars should be dodged. |
| **Commuting** | Taxi and local transport is habitual. Taxis are always with meter and in routine they don't charge extra. In local transport, day tickets are the simple and best for newcomers. It might cost little extra but stress-free during travel. |
| **Phone** | Business calls are answered by saying company name or own family name. Not by "Hello". |
| **Professional behavior** | Germans like their own space and do not expect step by step instructions on the project. They work independently and take responsibilities in a serious manner. |
| **Gifts** | Bring gifts from one's home town or country on business is not in fashion. But some Germans like it.<br><br>Acceptable gifts at business meetings are items of office equipment, pens with company's logo. |
| **Corruption** | Germany has very less corruption. Don't try to give any type of bribe. |

| Dinning | There can be many types of dining with business partners. In Restaurant, it could be possible that one have to pay his/her own bills (Individual bill) or one person pay bill for the complete. The dining starts with drinks, starters, main course, desserts and more drinks. It is not usual to share the dish. Water is not for free. Tipp in Restaurant, 5-10 % of the sum is normal. |

| WORKING | |
|---|---|
| **Looking for a Job** | Searching job, the best way to start looking for a job is over the Internet. Here are some famous ways:<br><br>• Federal Employment Agency<br><br>• Online job portals, Newspapers and Job fairs.<br><br>• Local employment agencies<br><br>• Apply directly to companies.<br><br>• Social Media like LinkedIn, Xing etc. |

| Application | Most important point is the quality of the application.<br><br>It includes:<br><br>• Covering letter<br><br>• Resume (good quality of resume photo is mandatory, don't paste passport photo)<br><br>• Certificates (Add translation certificate if the certificates language are not in German or English) |
|---|---|
| **Work Permits** | Nationals of EU, Liechtenstein and Switzerland are treated don't require work permits, however one must register the stay at local authorities. For non-European, obtaining a work permit can be slow and tedious process. |
| **Blue Cards** | Germany introduces "Blue Cards" as a new residence/work permit for highly skilled non-EU citizens and eases restrictions on foreign students studying at German universities.<br><br>• To qualify for the Blue Card an applicant must have a university degree and an employment contract with a German company that pays a salary of at least €47,600 per year (2014). |

| | |
|---|---|
| | • For certain occupations that suffer from shortages of skilled labor the salary level is €37,128 per year (2014). It belongs to engineers, qualified communications and technology experts, medical doctors and certain other fields. |
| | • The Blue Card may initially be valid for up to four years. (also depends on work contract) An application for an unlimited residence permit (Aufenthaltstitel) may be applied for after three years of Blue Card. If a Blue Card holder has B1 Level German language. He/she can apply for an unlimited residence permit after 2 years.<br><br>• Family members of a Blue Card holder are allowed to work in Germany. Spouses do not need German skills to join the Blue Card holder. |
| **Travel Outside for longer time** | Owners of the Blue card can stay outside the EU for maximum 12 months without losing the right of staying in Germany.<br><br>Owners of the blue card have the right, after having stayed in Germany for 18 months, to move to another country of European Union. |

| Citizenship | Germany provides dual citizenship but doesn't apply to Indian. Applicant must give up their Indian citizenship. |
|---|---|
| | • To be eligible for German citizenship, a person has to have lived legally in Germany for at least eight years. There are always some exceptional. |
| | • Foreigners who have successfully completed an integration course are after seven years. |
| | • Persons wishing to become citizens must also declare their allegiance to the Constitution. |
| | • Sufficient command of German language. Knowledge of German is an essential prerequisite for integration into our society. (Better than B2 Level) |
| | • Legal and social systems knowledge (by taking an integration course); |
| | • Applicants must be able to support themselves without recourse to social assistance or unemployment benefits (Arbeitslosengeld II). |

| | |
|---|---|
| | • Not committed any serious criminal offenses. |
| **Taxes** | Taxes on income may vary from 20% to 50%. There are many online tax calculator. Search as Brutto-Netto Rechner to calculate the net income. Following are type of Tax brackets:<br><br>• class I = single<br><br>• class II = single parent (living alone with the child/children)<br><br>• class III = married and the spouse has no income or lower income<br><br>• class IV = married and similar income to the spouse<br><br>• class V = opposite of class III, ie this is the class your lower earning spouse has if you have III<br><br>• class VI= for a second job or for deduction without proper employee information |
| **Social Security** | Followings are subject to social security contributions:<br><br>• Health insurance fund – it ensures the costs of visits to the doctor, and medication and therapy.<br><br>• Long-term care insurance - Offers basic insurance for the contingency of being dependent on long-term care owing to illness. |

| | |
|---|---|
| | • Pension insurance fund - A pension money after retirement. Basically, the amount of pension one receive depends on the income and the number of years one has worked in Germany.<br><br>• Accident insurance – It covers the costs of medical treatment and occupational rehabilitation after an accident at work.<br><br>• Unemployment insurance fund. |
| **kid's Allowance (Kindergeld)** | A taxpayer with children eligible for Kindergeld, whether employed, self-employed or independent. One can get it as a rule until the children turn 18. Parents get €184 per month for each of the first two children, €190 for the third child and €215 for each subsequent one. Allowances number are approximately and subjected to change. |
| **Travel to Company** | There is no pick up service from company or school. Public transport is generally used. Also, no uniform in school, office, college, etc. Campanies gets discounted tickets for employees yearly travel pass. |

| Unemployment | Unemployment benefits are paid if the person has no job and has worked for at least 12 months in the last two years. Benefits are around 60% to 67% of previous net salary and are paid directly into applicant. |
|---|---|
| **Church tax (Kirchensteuer)** | If one belong to Christianity and wants to register in church. Than he or she is liable to pay church tax. It is approximate 8% of the income tax. Being optional, one can formally deregister from the religious organization and this will also terminate the church tax. |
| **Dressing at office** | Business dress in Germany is understated, formal and conservative Also depends on company environment. Jeans and formal shirt works too. |
| **Dinning with colleagues** | • Do not start eating until the host starts or someone says "Guten Appetit" (have a nice meal).<br><br>• Beer and wine are part of a normal dinner and alcoholic drinks are usually offered to guests.<br><br>• Schnapps is a popular drink at the end of meals. |

| | |
|---|---|
| | • Do not insist on alcoholic drinks if a person has rejected your initial offer therefore, and do not order for them. A German who rejects a drink is not just being shy or polite but does not want to drink<br><br>• The most common toast with wine is "Zum Wohl!" and with beer is "Prost" (good health). |
| **Meetings** | • Meetings in German companies are generally scheduled well in advance.<br><br>• It is advisable to schedule appointments a few weeks beforehand by telephone or Emil. Brief preliminary meetings may sometimes be arranged at short notice.<br><br>• Don't give surprises in the meeting. It's advised to send pre-notice or pre-results to contact person.<br><br>• Try to avoid important business meetings in the months of July, August or December, as its vacation time. |

| Emails | • A clear, short and direct subject line is important. |
|---|---|
| | • Use professional salutations. *(Dear, Hello, Dr., Mr. Ms. Use only family name till we get familiar and getting acceptance to use the first name)* |
| | • Prefer to use simple English and vocabulary. |
| | • Be cautious with humor and emoticons. |
| | • Avoid sending continuous reminder Emails. |
| | • If it's urgent, mentioned clearly the deadline of required information. |
| **Integrate into office** | Try to be social in office, join the team for lunch. It helps to integrate quickly into the team. It is good to learn and speak German language to integrate into office. |

| STUDENTS | |
|---|---|
| **Universities** | Most of the universities are Government or public universities. There are 3 types of Universities:<br><br>1. TU – Technical University<br><br>2. Uni – University<br><br>3. FH – University of Applied Science |
| **G e r m a n Language** | There are courses in German as well as in English. English courses are 100% in English and Germany will be taught as an extra course. Mixed languages courses are also available. It is always beneficial to have German language skill. |
| **Courses** | The German Academic Exchange Service or DAAD (German: Deutscher Akademischer Austauschdienst) is the largest German support organization in the field of international academic co-operation. Most of the international courses are mentioned in DAAD website. |
| **Studying Method** | Studying type is the very practical base. Learning by heart might not be helpful. Some of the exams are open book which means students can bring their books with them for help. |

| Students Clubs | Multiple clubs or network groups are available. This helps international students to integrate and learn. |
|---|---|
| University Parties | Parties organized by universities are of world class. In Summer there are many open air festivals. Depends Live bands shows are also organized by universities. Alcohol drinks are also available to buy. |
| Hostels | Universities have their own Hostels. Generally the hostels are for both boys and girls. Individuals rooms are allotted and washroom, kitchen, livings rooms have to be shared. Food is not provided in hostels. Students have to cook by themselves. |
| Groups | Don't be in home country groups. It will create a problem to integrate with others country students. |
| Telephone Contracts | Be careful in taking the contract and use of the internet. It happens many times new students receive massive bills unknowingly. |
| Indian Food | Indian grocery is available in Indian stores and vegetables. Everyday grocery is available at Germany stores. In the small town where Indian stores are not available, use Indian online stores. |

| Travel | Student semester ticket for a limited region is provided at very economical price from the University. Purchasing train tickets a few weeks in advance can save you up to 50%. Ask about the "Spar-Preis" |
|---|---|
| Training | To apply for training, prepare resume as per German standard using good resume picture. Before apply, read the requirements carefully and explain the reasons of eligibility and interest for that training. Don't just shoot general resume to all applications. |
| Guidance | Be in contact with senior students and professor to seek guidance and further steps. |
| Part Time Jobs | Students are allowed to do full-time 90-day job or 180 part-time Job. Job related to education has no limit. Focus on students rather than odd jobs. Talk parts in universities research projects or social projects. |
| Academic Grades | German academic system is different than Indian.<br><br>General Notes are 1.0, 2.0, 3.0, 4.0 and 5.0. |

|  | There are sub levels too between levels like<br><br>1.3, 1.5 and 1.7.<br><br>• Note 1.0 (Excellent good) is the best possible grade and is given for outstanding performance<br><br>• Note 2.0 (Good) is is given for performance that meets the standard completely and is above-average.<br><br>• Note 3.0 (Satisfactory) indicates „average" performance.<br><br>• Note 4.0 (Sufficient) is the lowest passing grade and is given if the standard has been met but with some notable errors.<br><br>• Note 5.0 (Deficient or Fail) is failing grades and is given if the standard has not been met but the basics have been understood. |
| **Examination** | Maximum chances to appear for any subjects depend on university standards. |
| **Semester break** | Students are allowed to take semester break for industrial training or for further development. It requires approval from specific authorities. |

| | |
|---|---|
| **Scholarships** | Many scholarships are available. Students have to apply well in time and it is sometimes a long process. So plan studies according. International Erasmus Mundus programs are available for talented students which include good scholarships. |
| **Bank Account** | International Students have to open a blocked account, from which they can extract limited amount per month. It ensures the finances required for students. |
| **Job fair** | There is no campus selection method in Germany. There is multiple Job fair where students can interact with companies HR and can directly apply. On the other side, students can apply online and they get a response. |

| TRAVELERS | |
|---|---|
| **Tourism** | Germany is not a favorite destination for tourists. But it is beautiful and must visit places are mentioned in a previous chapter. |
| **Salute** | "Nazi Salute" or shouting "Heil Hitler" is a criminal offense and punishable up to 5 years of imprisonment. Evan doesn't joke on this topic. It's a taboo. Don't confuse Nazi symbol to Hindu Swastik symbol. Don't bring any product from India with Swastik symbol. |

| Transport | The best mode of transport is Train. It is fast and has good frequency. It will affect the pocket but worth to travel. Long distance bus travel recently started. They are of good choice and economic. Car sharing concept is also there, use at own risk. Some person cancels without informing in advance. Generally there are no "kuli" or helping service at railway stations. Take your luggage accordingly. |
|---|---|
| Toll Taxes | There are no Toll taxes in Germany. One can drive whole Germany free of toll. |
| Gas station | Gas stations on highways are little expensive but not too much. Food is damm expensive there. Self-service for filling the gas is common.<br><br>To use the toilet in a gas station, it can cost 70 cents per person. |
| Credit Cards | Credit cards are not as famous as in the US. So have some cash while traveling to remote areas. |
| Climate | Germany's climate varies region to region. North Germany's winter is cold and rainy. South Germany's winter are exceedingly cold and snowy. One can experience temperature from -10 °C to 35°C in a whole year. The most popular tourist months are from May to October. |

| Beverages | Beer is usually served in 0,3 (small) or 0,5 Liter sizes (large), although in some areas of Germany a 1-liter glass is also famous. |
|---|---|
| Smoking | In most parts of Germany smoking is not allowed in public buildings and inside restaurants or cafes. However there are „Raucherclubs", i.e. small pubs etc. where smoking is allowed. |
| Stammtisch | Many restaurants will have a table used by regulars from a company, society etc. Such tables will usually have a „Stammtisch" label. One can consider it as "Reserved". So ask before using them. |
| Service | Unlike other countries, customer service is often not a high priority in Germany. It is not in culture. In a hotel, don't expect to get escort service to the room. Generally in reception they will tell where the room is and explain about the room functions. Exceptions are always there. |
| Beaches | Nude beaches are mentioned as FKK (Freikörperkultur) which means free body culture. Topless girls are common in beaches. |
| M e d i c a l Insurance | Medical services are expensive, get a good health insurance before traveling to Germany. |
| Help | Need any help, just ask them. Most German speaks basic English and they are always happy to help. |

# 21. TIPS FOR GERMANS IN INDIA

India is country which has been divided into 29 states and 7 union territories, each with separate administrations and governed by a central administration. Customs can differ by state across the country. It will be a good idea to get some additional state-specific information in addition to the following information.

| GENERAL FOR ALL | |
|---|---|
| **Emergency Numbers** | All Over India- Police Control Room – 100, Fire Service – 101, Ambulance 102. Also many states have an ambulance service on 108<br><br>Women's Helpline -181, Child Helpline – 1098 |
| **German Missions in India** | In addition to the Embassy in New Delhi, there are German missions in Bangalore, Mumbai, Chennai and Kolkata and can be contacted in case of emergencies.<br><br>New Delhi- 44199199, Bangalore - +91-96325 42972, Chennai - + 91-4424301600, Mumbai -+91 9769485478, Kolkata -033-24791142 |

| | |
|---|---|
| **Hospitals or Doctors** | Most of the bigger cities have good hospitals with emergency services. Medical help in small towns and villages may be difficult to come by. Many hotels offer a doctor's service on call. |
| **Vaccinations** | Yellow fever vaccine is the only mandatory vaccine during International travel. While not mandatory WHO recommends the following vaccinations before visiting India – Adult Diphtheria & Tetanus, Hepatitis A, Hepatitis B, Typhoid, Polio, Varicella, Japanese B Encephalitis, Meningitis, Rabies and Tuberculosis. Remember them to take them two weeks before traveling. |
| **Medications** | It is safer to carry own prescription medication though most medication will be available in the bigger pharmacies. Always carry emergency supplies of Anti-diarrhea pills, Ibuprofen, Paracetamol and mosquito repellent cream. Mosquitoes and other insects are common. |
| **Police** | They are generally helpful to foreigners. May not be very fluent in English but helpful. |

| | |
|---|---|
| **Negotiating Traffic** | Motorists in India have a general disregard for traffic rules. Always take care when crossing the road even at a zebra crossing. Jumping signals is not uncommon. Keep your wits about you when on foot. Avoid hiring a self-driven car. Even Indians who have lived abroad for a few years are wary of driving when they return home. |
| **Weather** | Weather across India varies according to the region you are in. Check forecasts for specific regions. The Himalayan states can be cold and snow bound at higher altitudes for a good part of the year. In the South, most places are hot for a good part of the year. Some places in the South can be cool during winter. Northern Plains have extreme temperatures, cold in winter, blazing hot in summer. Carry plenty of sun block. Monsoons can be difficult in many states. Make sure to carry umbrellas if traveling during the monsoons. Some cities can be particularly difficult with a lot of water logging in the streets. Monsoon is also the time when infectious diseases are rampant. |

| First Day | In some cities like Chennai or Bangalore, it is easy to get by with English, however for most parts of India, keep a phrase book handy. In the Northern states, one would need to carry a Hindi phrasebook and in the Southern states, one would need to carry a phrase book of the local language – there are four different languages in the South. If you are traveling during summer, make sure that you take it easy on the first day. The heat can be taxing. Keep well hydrated and keep sunblock handy. |
|-----------|-----------|
| Clothes | Cities are more liberal about the kind of attire wear. In smaller towns try not to expose too much flesh as it is culturally frowned upon. That apart, the sun is harsh in most parts of the country in summer and it would be safer not to expose yourself to direct sunlight. Most Europeans who make the mistake of thinking that they can pick up a tan run the risk of falling sick. |
| Footwear | Don't wear footwear inside places of worship. It should be left in a designated stand outside the Temple or Gurudwara or Mosque. When visiting homes, ask if footwear needs to be left out, as this is the custom in most Indian homes. |

| **Personal Talk** | Asking personal questions are common. Don't be offended or surprised if someone ask about marital or family status. Many may even expect this from others as they consider it being friendly. Even a taxi driver getting chummy and can ask about private life. |
|---|---|
| **Non-Vegetarian Food** | Non-vegetarian food is available in most states but Hindus do not eat beef and Muslims do not eat pork. Some restaurants serve only vegetarian food, a few serve both. Chicken, fish and mutton are more commonly available. The egg is also considered non-vegetarian. Purely vegetarian restaurants are famous in India. |
| **Street Food** | Want to have adventurous spicy food, try street food. Hygiene is not a strong point. |
| **Drinking Water** | Play it safe and stick to drinking bottled mineral water. Check the seal on bottle before use. In summers make sure to keep well hydrated and watch out for any sign of dehydration. |
| **Greeting** | Traditional greeting is in the form of a Namaste which a greeting with palms held together at face level. |

| Kissing in Public | This is an absolute taboo. Indian culture frowns upon kissing in public. Some states are more accepting lately but the safest thing to do is to avoid it. Public displays of affection can even invite censure from the police. |
|---|---|
| Stray Animals | Indians believe in non-violence towards all their fellow creatures but this results in a lot of stray animals on the road. Cows, horses, dogs all vie for space with vehicles. Avoid befriending stray animals as they may carry diseases. Take care not to get too close to street dogs. Rabies is a very real risk in India.<br><br>Monkeys are another source of trouble in India. In some places they try to snatch bags in search of food. Avoid feeding the stray animals as they are not tame. |
| Public Transport | Some of the major cities are well linked by the metro however in most other places you can rely on a three-wheeler – the autorickshaw. Be prepared to haggle, though they are supposed to run on meter, many will not. App-based taxi services have become common in the recent years in many of the bigger cities. Public buses are difficult in most Indian cities for the foreign traveler and are best avoided. |

| Safety | Play it safe and avoid wandering around alone, especially after dark. Take care of own belongings. Pickpockets are common in crowded places in most cities. Be wary of beggars who might sidle up. |
|---|---|
| **Drugs** | Possession of drugs is illegal in India. |
| **Public Toilets** | Public toilets are best avoided. In an emergency look for the nearest hotel. |
| **Power Cuts** | Power cuts are still common in many cities. Though most places are now equipped with backup power, do carry a torch for emergencies. |

| BUSINESS TRAVELLERS | |
|---|---|
| **Dressing** | The formal business attire of suits is common especially among those higher on the corporate rung. Women in business suits are acceptable though formal wear for Indian women is the Saree or in recent times Salwaar Kameez. Ensure that the skirt for business is not overly short. |
| **Punctuality** | While most Indians have a laid back attitude to time, punctuality is valued for business meetings. |
| **Greetings** | While a Namaste is the traditional Indian greeting, a firm handshake is common in the corporate sector. |

| Business Meetings | Business meetings may be preceded with casual chit-chat. Exchanging visiting cards is common. |
|---|---|
| Gifts | Indians often carry small gifts while traveling. It might be a good idea to do the same. Chocolates are generally appreciated. Small mementos from Germany will be well received. |
| Dining | Western culture as penetrated most business circles in India and dining can be accompanied with drinks. Many of the bigger/higher-end hotels serve alcohol. However invited to a home, there could be a chance that drinks do not accompany the meal. Beer is also considered non family drink and may not be served in family parties. Eating with fingers is acceptable as it is a local custom. Indian food can be spicy. Avoid overdoing it if it is the first time. |

| TRAVELLING WITH CHILDREN ||
|---|---|
| Food | Traveling with an infant, make sure to carry enough of preferred baby formula milk. |
| Medication | Carry all child's necessary medications. Diarrhea in young children can be particularly dangerous, take care of it immediately. |

| Child Seats | Don't expect to find child seats in cars and taxis. |
|---|---|
| Crowds | Keep an eye on kids and hold on tight, especially in marketplaces and other public spaces. The crowds can be daunting. Most places in India are crowded. |
| Health | Keep children well hydrated. The heat can be very deceptive. |
| Culture | Indians are very fond of children. Europeans are likely to attract some attention, most of it curious and positive. Be polite but firm about excessive touching. |

| TRAVELLERS WITH DISABILITIES | |
|---|---|
| Accommodation | Higher end hotels are wheel-chair friendly but might not find that to be the case with the lower end hotels or public places. |
| Accessibility on Streets | Streets and roads are not disabled friendly. Ramps in public places are present in some of the newer constructions but most however will have steps. Elevators are present but not all buildings have elevators that are large enough to accommodate wheelchairs. |

| Transport | Most public transport like buses is not disabled friendly. The best option is to hire a car. Make sure to call ahead and ensure that the vehicle has space to store wheelchair. |
|---|---|

| LONE WOMEN TRAVELLERS | |
|---|---|
| Clothing | Wear comfortable clothes, do not expose too much flesh, it might attract unwanted attention |
| Safety | Always carry a cell phone. Be careful while dealing with men, especially those who are less educated. India has received a lot of negative publicity on women's safety. While some of these could be exaggerations, always play it safe and avoid going out alone after dark. Hire taxis recommended by police or good hotel. |
| Jewelry | Keep jewelry to a safe place. |
| Behaviour | Act confident and don't give out personal information to anyone however friendly they might appear. Always inform friends or hotel about travel plan. Keep the acquaintances and friends informed regarding whereabouts. If stared at by unwanted men, just ignore them and walk on. |

| STUDENTS | |
|---|---|
| **Accommodation** | Make sure about safe and good accommodation sorted out before arrival to India. |
| **Clothing** | Many Universities in India have regulations regarding suitable on campus clothing. Refer to the respective University guides for this. |
| **Respect for Professors** | Indian culture does not permit addressing teachers and professors by their first names. Sir/Ma'am is the norm in most Universities. |

Printed in the United States
By Bookmasters